Sass Mouth

DESTINY IS A JOKE

A memoir
by
Jacki Kane

*Dan,
Thanks for being so nice about my book. Can't wait to read yours. Tennis cans are in!
Jacki Kane*

Author's Note: This is a memoir that draws from my memory and personal truths. To convey the truth as I remember it while protecting the identities of the people involved, all names, locations and identifying characteristics have been changed.

© 2009 Jacki Kane. All rights reserved.

This book, or parts thereof, may not be reproduced in any form without permission. The scanning, uploading, and distribution of this book via the Internet or via any other means without the permission of the author is illegal and punishable by law. Please purchase only authorized electronic editions, and do not participate in or encourage electronic piracy of copyrighted materials.
Your support of the author's rights is appreciated.

The Library of Congress has catalogued this edition as follows:
Kane, Jacki
Sass Mouth, Destiny is a Joke / Jacki Kane
ISBN #: 978-0-557-13520-2
Memoir

"When they're little,

they step on your toes.

When they're big,

they walk on your heart."

∽ My mother

To my savior Sam

and my two Samlets,

who rescue my heart every day

CONTENTS

1	The Green Room	1
2	Freeze! Police-Mom	5
3	Happy Valley	11
4	Colonial Elementary	15
5	Open Mic Night	21
6	Twinkle, Twinkle Little Child Star	31
7	Bad Jackie	47
8	Solo Flyer	55
9	The Truth List Hurts	65
10	The Last Doublemint Twin	73
11	Preteen Criminal Confidential	83
12	Sex Party	93
13	Busted	103
14	The Heckler Comeback	111
15	The "I Hate Jacki" Show	123
16	Kid War	131
17	The Bomb	139
18	Lois Lane	147
19	The Glass Heart	159
20	Metal Door	173
21	One Last Try	183

Jacki Kane

> "My friends say I'm sarcastic.
> Like I really value their opinions."

1. THE GREEN ROOM

Looking at the audience from behind the stage was like popping out of a manhole in the path of a semi. At that moment, I would have preferred a truck over the 250 people sitting there waiting to be entertained. Blinding stage lights forced my eyes to squeeze into pinholes, and a thick cottony blanket of smoke hung over the audience. Only the first row of the audience looked like people. The rest were just silhouettes. Behind me, other graduates of the Dave Parson's School of Comedy fumbled around the Green Room at the Yuk It Up Club in Atlanta waiting to perform their sets for the first time.

Everyone dissolved into a silent nervous hum similar to standing too close to an electric box as Dave Parsons, our comedy teacher, made his way out to the microphone. A veteran of stand-up comedy, Dave had once pierced through the national arena, then settled back to a local celebrity, running a comedy school and doing stand-up at corporate gigs. I ducked back inside the curtain as Dave started his banter. Tom and Sarah slid closer together on a boxy brown loveseat as if they were freezing cold. Dan smoothed his hair back while mashing a bar straw flat with his teeth.

"Okay, let's bring out our first graduate," Dave said as everyone in the Green Room looked up, eyes wide as plates. "Give it up for Dan Sandborn." Dan moved swiftly over to the curtain, shook the nervousness from his body like a wet dog, and walked proudly on stage. For Dan, performing stand-up was a lifelong dream. Other classmates said their friends put them up to it. I told everyone I just wanted to be successful at something. But the truth was, instead of overcoming my dangerously low self-esteem and creating the life that I wanted, I expected someone else to do it for me. Usually, I recruited boyfriends to save me. But this time, comedy would be my prince. One smooch of stardom would magically transform me from corporate executive wannabe to hip, funny chick. I dreamed about a higher version of myself - someone who wore trendy clothes, won awards for writing, and amazed everyone with her razor-sharp wit. But the distance between dream and reality seemed wider than the Grand Canyon.

Hip was a word for cowgirls and girls named Bianca, not me. My friends called me "Lands' End." To me, growing up in a Baltimore suburb meant blindly following a preppy code that required wearing at least one item with a whale, duck, or sea shell at all times. On graduation night, I tried to look like a stand-up comic by wearing a red and black iridescent vintage tux jacket. But abandoning my pink and green mallard duck outfit made me nervous. What if I tripped the alarm in Baltimore that sounded when a preppy defector got loose south of the Mason-Dixon line? Would my father still love me if I stopped wearing khakis? Just in case, I wore the preppy standard: penny loafers.

As for winning awards, I wasn't even doing the kind of writing I set out to do when I moved to Atlanta in the first place. Instead of following my dream of becoming Holly Hunter in *Broadcast News* (I even owned a smart Velcro bow that gift wrapped nearly any outfit.), I chickened out of a $13,000 "video jockey" job at CNN and settled for a safe corporate marketing job at a muffler company. Investigative reporting there meant exploring the dynamics of exhaust fumes in the company magazine. And, my sharp wit was dulled down by the stifling control of corporate management. But comedy would change all that. I just knew it.

My set was next to last. As I waited, I pressed my back against the wall and listened carefully to every set-up-punchline of each comic's set so I would know exactly how many words away I was from disaster. One by one, each graduate burst through the curtain in triumph. In a last-minute fit of desperation, I scrawled key words from my set on my palm. But my hands sweat so badly, only a smudge remained. "Okay, ladies and gentlemen," Dave boomed as my buddy Gene bounded through the curtain, looking exhilarated as if he just got off a roller coaster. I gave him a quick high-five and edged closer to the stage.

"This next comic has been performing in Waffle Houses across Georgia," Dave announced. The audience roared. Cool, I wrote that. Oh no, I'm next. Then, Gene karate chopped my back, saying, "You can do it, Jack. You're the Comedy Babe." That's what my classmates called me, Comedy Babe.

As Dave announced: "Please give a big hand for Jacki Eberstarker," my mother's voice rang out in my head: "You dumb-ass bitch, you'll never pull this off." After five years of therapy, I thought I had overcome any previously scheduled programming from my mother. Messages like those usually penetrated my confidence like poison darts and paralyzed me. But this time, my body jerked into autopilot, yanked the red curtain open, and walked itself on stage.

The lights were so blinding, I could only hear my roommate Trixie in the front row, screaming, "Go Eberstarker, woo!" After living in Atlanta with a variety of roommates, Trixie was my best roommate and friend yet. A classically trained singer nicknamed after Speed Racer's girlfriend, Trixie understood the anxiety of performing and cheered me on every step of the way through comedy school. When I scrunched my eyebrows to find her underneath the smoke, the audience laughed harder. Later, when I looked at the videotape, I realized why. My eyes rolled around in my head like black marbles in saucers of milk - one of those '50s black enamel cat clocks with the swinging tail. As I waited for the laughter to die down, the Rules of Comedy rang out in my head. *Don't walk on laughs.* So I waited longer for the audience to get even quieter.

"Turns out Eberstarker's German. It means to urinate on a mountain." The audience exploded, making me back off the microphone in surprise. Oh, no. I broke Rule #2: *Never back away from the audience because it makes you seem unsure of yourself and throws the door open for hecklers.* Oh great, I forgot to write canned heckler comebacks like: "Hey, do I bother you when you're flipping burgers at McDonald's?" Everyone I knew was in the audience. I hoped they wouldn't heckle me.

"Guess that explains why our family tree is...Dead." Somehow my body delivered the set while my mind kept running through the rules of comedy.

"I'm still wearing a training bra...Don't know what they're training for." Another eruption. "Maybe they'll be ready for the Olympics." More applause.

Good, following the believability rule worked: Don't tell the audience something they couldn't possibly fathom, like a gorgeous woman telling jokes about how she can't get dates. First of all, I'd collapse like a marionette if someone called me gorgeous. "Cute" was the adjective reserved for me. Cindy Brady was cute, damn it. Obviously, my flat chest was completely believable.

"I've been in therapy to get over my fear of being trapped in a box...With a mime." I knocked on the air like a mime, making the audience howl.

"Mimes are actually clowns that couldn't make the cut." Trixie's dead-on Scooby Doo laugh pierced through the applause and almost made me lose my place.

"But clowns are what I really hate. So I started an anti-clown activist group... No Boz." The audience liked this joke better. So I waited for them to slow down.

"Now they're after me. They're showing up at my house...picketing. Looked out my window yesterday. This Volkswagen Beetle pulled up and like 2000 clowns piled out." Another solid laugh.

"My parents thought I had a short attention span, so they sent me to Our Lady of Perpetual Guilt. The school motto was: Pay attention or go to hell." The audience fell out, chalking up another score for the final comedy rule: Save the funniest for last. I thanked the audience, handed Dave the microphone, and walked off-stage while they were still laughing. "Jacki Eberstarker, everybody," Dave said. "Okay, you guys have been great. Just one more victim left, folks."

I floated through the curtain to the Green Room, numb from the kind of high that gets people arrested. The other graduates jumped to their feet: "You killed!" Gene slapped my back, "I told ya you were the Comedy Babe." I was thrilled to find a new obsession, not to mention a handy way to battle my demons by bringing them to light on stage. Making 250 people laugh hysterically about my life felt like loosening one foot out of the grappling hooks of my past. I was on my way toward becoming the New Jacki. Little did I know that comedy was about to force new truths to the surface like rats in a flood. I had yet to discover one unwritten rule of comedy: *Don't use humor to cover up your innermost fears. Everyone will know, and they'll eat you alive.*

> "My mother wore the apron, the pants,
> and the gun belt in the family."

2 . FREEZE! POLICE-MOM

The wind blasted through the open window of our silver Chevelle as my mother launched a high-speed chase through our peaceful suburban Baltimore neighborhood. Other mothers wore platform sandals and carried straw purses. My mother sported steel-toed tactical shoes and packed a .38. Fresh from graduating from the police academy in 1975, she tucked her "Pat Eberstarker" name badge and county police badge in her purse, just in case. She was convinced crimes were constantly in progress, and that it was her duty to apprehend every criminal. Personally.

Technically we were undercover, disguised as a plain-clothes family returning from Fashion Quarter Mall. My 6-year-old brother, Bruce, and 4-year-old brother, Matt, dangled their pencil legs in the back seat. I rode shotgun, like a partner. We rounded a corner as the racing stripes of the red Pontiac GTO zipped through an intersection.

"Speeding bastard," our mother growled, as she squealed wheels after the car. As we rocketed past houses, neighbor kids froze in mid-play like child mannequins in a Sears catalog. The Pontiac screamed up a big hill on Happy Valley Road while I dreamed of being a pre-teen version of *Police Woman*, tossing my hair like Pepper and mashing my lips together, pretending they were frosted with gloss. When our mother performed a law-abiding stop behind the sign, looked both ways, then floored the Chevelle up the hill, my brothers cheered, "Wooo!" until she barked: "You two, shut the hell up."

When we caught up with the Pontiac, she flashed the high beams wildly, waving her gun and badge out the window. Only then did the Pontiac roll to a reluctant stop. Officer Eberstarker slammed the door behind her as we shuffled around making room for the guy, thinking there'd be an arrest. But all she did was talk nicely to him after all that because she was unable to issue a ticket since we were outside Ball County city limits where she worked as a police officer.

Back in the car, she switched the high beams off and spat, "Asshole." Other kids in this situation perhaps would've sensed the quiet rumble of my mother's anger and kept their mouths shut. Not me. After earning a "1" on my third grade report card for outstanding progress in oral communication, I mistakenly thought I was supposed to verbalize things clearly not meant to be said. Squaring my shoulders, I delivered what I thought was a smart question: "Aren't you going to arrest him?"

"Shut the hell up, you stupid little bitch," said my mother. "Or I'll shut you up."

I slid to the bottom of the bucket seat, stared at the silver cursive "Chevelle" emblem on the glove compartment, then whispered to my Bionic Woman doll the rest of the day.

The relationship between my mother and me was like the relationship between the mole and mallet in a Whak-a-Mole game: whenever I surfaced from a hole, she pummeled me. But sometimes my buck-toothed spirit would pop up again, triumphant, only to be hammered back down again. The results were mixed. Sometimes I'd feel permanently flattened and sink into a depressive hole for weeks. But as I got older, I'd find strong-willed friends who pierced my mother's tough façade and stared at her straight, daring her to attack them too. She never tried. Seeing my mother temporarily reduced fueled me with the confidence I needed to furiously pop up in different holes, confusing her and rendering her mallet useless.

Opinions vary about which one of her children my mother disliked the most. I contend she despised me the most consistently, which turned out to be a good thing. Kids who are loved one minute then despised the next must be totally confused. At least I knew where I stood because she exploded at my every move. But still, hope that she would change her mind about me appeared to me as randomly as noticing a sparkle of dust in a ray of sunshine. Any hope vanished after the afternoon she walked the runway of a charity fashion show at my school with another little girl.

It started when, after noticing other mothers volunteering in my third grade class, I asked mine why she never did. She seemed to soften for a moment, and to my surprise, started appearing as a class helper and fundraiser organizer. To the outside world she must have looked like a mother who cared deeply about her children. But this was a woman who forced her kids to line up at parties, saluting her as cocktail-wielding guests shifted uncomfortably in their seats.

Now, volunteering for the fashion show at my school, I didn't know what to expect. I wasn't surprised that other girls in my class were picked to be in the fashion show, since I was sure my mother was right - I thought I was too ugly. But nothing prepared me for the sight of my mother sashaying down the runway holding the hand of a "model" daughter - a daughter who wasn't me. Pretty and smiling, each of them took careful steps and nodded to the audience as I went ballistic.

How come she's nice to that little girl?

My grandmother held me tighter, mumbling, "Oh, I knew this would happen." Adults around me pleaded, "Oh honey, you're just upset because you wanted to be in the show."

But the truth was, I believed my mother when she told me I was ugly and stupid and a flat-out terrible kid. Now she had found a replacement with way cuter hair and smarter clothes that she obviously liked better.

Throughout my life, the emptiness of not having experienced a nurturing, maternal love would stun me at the most random times, like when someone else's mother told me to carry a purse that "matches, not clashes" with my shoes. Moments like those made me feel as out of place as showing up at a formal wearing cut-off shorts and a t-shirt. Moments like those, I found myself paralyzed with a "You're not like the other girls" terror running through me.

And yet, no matter how much my mother disliked me, as her child, I was enormously proud of her. She succeeded at becoming a female police officer at a time when hardly any officers were women. Plus, it was pretty cool knowing that our mother was the only one on field trips packing heat. Soon our house transformed from daycare to outpost. She constantly monitored a CB as it blared in the kitchen. Small handguns suddenly appeared in drawers and a shotgun leaned against the wall in the upstairs closet. She seemed happy at first to shed her stay-at-home mom status. Eventually, she'd turn her police missives internally. Instead of being on a mission to find out who spilled Kool-Aid on the counter, she focused on crime prevention at home.

Convinced the word "child" was interchangeable with "criminal" and that her children were destined for cover profiles in "Penitentiary Life Magazine," she set out to stop us before we headed for our inevitable lives of hard crime. But instead of using friendly childhood icons we could relate to, like explaining that *The Cat in the Hat* should have been charged for breaking and entering, or Mister Magoo arrested for driving under the influence, she forced us to watch real convicts on *Scared Straight*. Had we been past the ages of 9, 6, and 4, our introduction to crime probably would have been more productive. At 9, I was too busy watching *Emergency!* and imitating Randolph Mantooth's eyebrows in the mirror to stage a hit on the Good Humor truck. Bruce and Matt were so involved baking dog turds in my Easy-Bake Oven, they weren't planning to roll some kid for his Pet Rock.

Dad, on the other hand, was the complete opposite. Pat Eberstarker screamed; George Eberstarker barely talked. She hated her kids; he adored his kids. She was explosive; he was comatose. Professionally, she handled disasters as they happened; he handled the aftermath. But one thing was for sure: We knew he loved us. He packed our sandwiches every day, toted popsicles home on his lunch break when we were sick, and scooped us up in the middle of the night when we were scared. In the summer, he chased us around the yard with our friends for hours until the lightning bugs whipped us in the face. My friends wanted a dad like ours; I wanted a mom like theirs. Sometimes, he crossed the line and became one of us kids, joining in our battle against our mother and forming a kind of "I Hate Mom Club."

Working shifts meant my mother slept for long periods of time, giving us ample opportunity to slip out of the house without her. By the time Dad got home, she was well into hibernation, preparing for her night shift. We piled into the 1972 Chevrolet Impala station wagon my parents called "Ironside" and drifted backwards down the driveway so she wouldn't wake up. Then Dad drove us to the Charred Grill Diner, where we immediately launched into our re-enactment of a TV commercial that was running constantly advertising Steak-Ums, thin sheets of unidentified meat just perfect for sub sandwiches.

The spot featured a family sitting around a table at a restaurant politely giving a waitress their order. When our Charred Grill Diner waitress arrived, Dad scooted back in the squeaky vinyl booth in nervous anticipation as we sat up straight, held our laminated menus up high, and started our act.

"I'll have a steak sandwich," Bruce tipped his blonde head back and stated proudly.

"I'll have a steak sandwich with cheese," Matt said, with a cheeky grin through his smudged face. He was one of those constantly dirty kids like Linus of the Peanuts. Except he was as dusty as the blanket.

"I'll have a steak sandwich with cottage cheese," I finished, popping up in my chair just like the pig-tailed girl with braces on the commercial when I said "cottage." My father slapped the linoleum table wheezing from laughing so hard.

"Oh, I get it. Steak Ums commercial, right?" Our completely unimpressed waitress cracked her gum and held her pen in mid air. "But is that what you really want?"

After cracking up at Matt bouncing his hotdog around and making it bark, we begged to stay out later to avoid going home and running into our mother.

"But she'll make us go to bed early before she goes to work. I hate her," I whined, setting off my father.

"Don't talk about your mother like that," he said, popping his straw down into his empty glass.

"Why?" I said, shocked at his reaction.

"Because she's your mother. You're supposed to love your mother," he demanded, then slid out of the booth.

When we got home, our mother leaned against the kitchen counter, smoking a cigarette in full uniform with one hand on her gun belt. "You got dinner without me, didn't you?" she demanded as she smashed her Virginia Slim into an ashtray and broke it clean in half like a kneeling scarecrow. As he stood in silence looking at her, she pounded her steel-toed shoes into the kitchen floor and slammed the back door so hard, the glass rattled. The three of us froze, looking to Dad for some kind of reaction. But instead of soothing the situation with a wise parental lesson, he said: "Want to watch *Emergency!?*" with the same kind of mischievous glint as if he had announced: "Hey kids, wanna blow up a banana with an M-80?" Just then, the Chevelle peeled wheels out of the driveway and spit gravel clear across Happy Valley Road.

> *"My childhood was so pathetic...*
> *Barbie stuck her head in my Easy Bake Oven."*

3 . HAPPY VALLEY

Early one Saturday, I padded down the thick-carpeted stairs of our colonial-style house to a brand new box of Alpha Bits and dug out the special prize before Bruce and Matt woke up. When I ripped the powder-covered wrapper open, a button rolled out. Michael Jackson's face popped out in a dome in the middle and type around the outside clearly stated: "Just call my name, and I'll be there." Really? Since *Land of the Lost,* my favorite show, wasn't on yet, I figured now was the right time to put this statement to the test. Jamming the button into my shorts pocket, I headed outside where the glistening white sidewalks tethered the houses together all across Happy Valley.

Before I called Michael Jackson's name, I froze in terror wondering what I would do if he actually showed up on the sidewalk? Would I have to kiss him? I didn't want to kiss him, just have a pint-sized celebrity to play with who can bust a move right here in Happy Valley. But after flailing my arms around screaming "Michael" for twenty minutes, my patience was giving way to pure rage because he plainly said he'd be there, but he wasn't. Just then, the special Alpha Bits prize popped out of my pocket and spun around to a stop on the sidewalk like a tin space ship. So technically, I did call him, and he showed up.

In an instant, a profound realization hit me: If you wait long enough, promises come true. So it's all Michael Jackson's fault that I believed my father when he told me the Mormon Tabernacle was Disney World, Brach Candies were set out by the store manager "just for good children," and savage bees from Africa were attacking Baltimore. The fact that we didn't fall for everything my father said was a pure miracle. We sensed *'Twas the Night Before Christmas* did not involve an industrial accident and were suspicious enough not to get caught stealing Brach Candies red-handed. It would have saved my parents thousands if they could have passed off the Mormon Tabernacle for Disney though. And, instead of realizing my mother hated almost everybody, I clung to the one time she kneeled down and said, "Of course I love you, you're the only little girl I have," and ignored how she then snapped, "Now get your God damned socks off my floor, you idiot." Waiting on my mother to demonstrate the love she claimed ran thin for me at an early age. Realizing that I wasn't the only one she hated, unfortunately, did not. Instead, I believed she hated only me, and I deserved it, which was both true and false.

By the time I jammed the Michael Jackson pin back in my pocket, the sidewalks were in full swing with Bruce riding his bike and Matt racing toward me, furiously pumping his tricycle pedals, failing to notice Jimmy Fragtonis from next door perched at the top of the neighbor's steep driveway on his bike. Jimmy lifted his feet up and let his bike coast down the driveway, building up speed, ramming Matt's tricycle, and knocking him flat across the sidewalk like a speed bump. Then, Jimmy intentionally ran over Matt's tadpole-size belly, leaving a thick black tire mark. A stunned Matt stayed flat on his back wailing, while I ran home to get help. My mother was already on her way, tearing down the sidewalk towards Matt. I told her what happened, and she picked up Matt with his striped t-shirt pulled up over his belly revealing the tire mark, and headed directly to the Fragtonis' house.

A fight immediately erupted between Jimmy's mother, Macy, and my mother with a completely non-apologetic Macy stomping after my mother down the sidewalk, screaming, "You'd better shut the hell up, or I'll shove that bike up your ass." Macy got the last word as my mother plopped Matt on the back porch, where he sat red-faced, trying to catch his breath, but was unhurt. I sat next to Matt with my Bionic Woman doll clamped to my chest to shield her bionic ear from such language. Bruce walked his bike back behind the house with the color drained out of his normally ruddy cheeks. Behind the sliding glass door, we could see our mother smoking a cigarette and furiously mopping the kitchen floor. I counted the hours, then minutes until Dad came home.

My father sometimes worked Saturdays and had already left. So we were alone with my mother and another shaky day. When we were with him, she went away, refusing to join in any family activity. When we were bad, she still screamed at us and smacked us around when he was home. When we were on our best behavior and having a good time, she still got incensed. We couldn't win.

When the floor was gleaming clean and dry, my mother announced lunch. We reluctantly went inside and sat down. Then, just as she had finished cleaning up lunch, Matt tipped a full pitcher of Kool-Aid into a cup, but forgot to turn the top to the open position, popping the top off and sending a red cascade splashing onto the floor. Oblivious, he took one gulp as my mother charged after him with fists balled, arms straight, and head down like a gymnast approaching a vault. She let him have it for what seemed like twenty minutes. And since every window in the house was open, her screams must have halted the entire neighborhood.

As she howled at him and jerked him sideways across the floor, suddenly the doorbell stopped her cold. She plopped a wailing Matt on the carpet and threw open the door as if she was about to attack someone. But a Baltimore County police officer stood there, hat in hand. She immediately straightened up her back and softened her shoulders.

"We received a noise complaint. A neighbor heard screaming and was concerned someone was hurt over here," he said. My mother pointed to Matt, sitting stunned on the carpet in his Charlie Brown striped shirt with his blonde hair tousled and a tell-tale crusty red Kool-Aid moustache. I hid nervously behind a chair, feeling sorry again for Matt and bracing for the worst.

"He spilled Kool-Aid all over the kitchen floor, and I just mopped it." She sounded dangerously indignant at first, then switched on her sing-song sweet voice she used when she talked to friends or first answered the phone. It's always been astounding to me how quickly she could throw the mean-nice switch. I hoped that he'd take her to jail so our dad would come home early. "I guess I just got carried away, Officer. You know how kids can get to you." She appeared as charming as Mrs. Brady and laughed all the way through the sentence as if they knew each other. Then he laughed, too, and the whole situation was over just like that. I couldn't believe what I was seeing.

"Alright, I'll let your neighbor know everything is okay over here," he said, ducking back out of the doorway.

She thanked the nice officer for his time and politely closed the front door. Switching her face from Stepford wife to Wicked Witch, she spun around and used a growling voice that sounded more like a man's, "That bitch, Macy. I'll get her for calling the police on me." She had her first target lined up, then turned to me. "And as for you, young lady, why did you let him in my kitchen when you know I just mopped the floor? And how could you just stand there when that Fragtonis brat ran over Matt?" Because I was the oldest, she constantly held me responsible for whatever my brothers did, whether they talked back or decorated a wall with her lipstick.

As tears stung my eyes, she slapped the back of my head and yelled, "You want something to cry about? I'll give you something to cry about," then shoved me toward the stairs, snapping my head back like a Rock 'em, Sock 'em Robot. I see-sawed between rage at constantly being blamed for everything and the desperation of complete helplessness. Her anger settled on me like rain on parched soil. Some got through the cracks and made its way to deeper levels. But because I knew my Dad loved me, some simply evaporated in the very heat she created. The rest of the afternoon, I waited for the sound of my Dad's station wagon being gently pulled into the driveway.

> "Some games are hard to play with imaginary playmates...
> Like dress up."

4 . COLONIAL ELEMENTARY

With summer officially over and the air getting crisp, the incidents with Macy Fragtonis stopped since our windows were closed and we quit playing outside. My mother switched to day shift, which meant fewer opportunities to get in a row with Macy. As the official site of such historical events as the writing of *The Star-Spangled Banner,* Baltimore bustled with bicentennial celebrations and red, white, and blue merchandise. Revolutionary re-enactments were all the rage. For my sixth grade year at Colonial Elementary, Dad bought me red, white, and blue socks to match my Revolutionary War hero pocket folders. Even more exciting, my tenth birthday was closing in, coincidentally as the 8-track was making way for the cassette recorder, and I wanted in on the action.

One night, my father returned home with a mysterious gray box, igniting my curiosity that it might contain audio-visual equipment. As he peeled off his London Fog trench coat revealing his still-crisp Oxford shirt, I hovered around the gray box, salivating. At the time, I was so obsessed by AV equipment that I'd avoid flossing in hopes that the dental hygienist would demonstrate proper technique using her filmstrip projector. All through dinner, I bugged Dad to open it. Finally, he shook his head with an, "Okay, okay."

Throwing open the hinged lid, he curled the oily filmstrip around the metal sprocket, gently touched the needle down on the record and headed to watch TV as I sat mesmerized by the advances of '70s technology.

The first frame featured a portrait of a very Beaver Cleaver-looking family: Suzie, the mom, smartly attired in a house dress. Ray, the dad, sported a business suit. Daughter Jane stood proudly in a pink cardigan sweater set, pearls, and hair band with her brother Steve in a varsity v-neck sweater and khakis. The voiceover on the cassette warmly introduced them: "The Smiths were one, big happy family, until one day. Beep." I flipped to the next frame. "Ray is tragically killed in a car accident, leaving Suzie and the kids penniless. Beep." The next frame revealed a harried Suzie bagging groceries with Steve and Jane in the background, hanging out with a crowd of hoods, wearing leather and smoking cigarettes. The concerned voiceover suddenly shifted to a warm, reassuring tone: "But it doesn't have to be this way…A life insurance policy can help." Just as the sales pitch started, it hit me: Time to launch my campaign to score AV equipment for my birthday.

Talking about tape recorders non-stop worked beautifully. On my birthday, I scored a black Sanyo tape recorder with a pop-up cassette lid and sliding handle. At first, I focused my efforts on recording "The Hustle" off my digital radio alarm clock. But my mother's screaming turned the recording into "Do the…God damn it you little assholes." My best friend, Ellie Gambit, who got a bright-red Sony tape recorder that looked like a purse, experienced the same thing with her mother. So at the time, I thought constant maternal howling was a normal parenting technique deployed in every household in America. Apparently, so did Ellie.

One day, we decided to tape our mothers, then compare whose mother screamed the loudest. Finding someone else who had a loud, violent mother made me feel like my situation was totally normal and a lot less scary. Somehow, that made my mother's behavior something we could have fun with, instead of be terrorized by. My mother's constant badgering had long since cancelled that part of me that craved nurturing. Her anger had become a kind of sound that droned on the way the refrigerator in the kitchen does – the constant murmur you never notice is there, until the power goes out. On some level, Ellie and I must have known that there was something dreadfully wrong with our mothers because we toted our recorders into the office of the Colonial Elementary School guidance counselor, Miss Larsen, and played our tapes for her.

Our "open space" school featured wall-to-wall carpet and partitions that formed a kind of maze, but no interior walls. Colonial Elementary was unlike any other school in the Baltimore County system. After failing miserably, this open school format would be labeled the most expensive experiment in Baltimore County history. Since then, walls have been installed like every other school. So much carpet blanketed every inch of the school, shuffling your feet on the floor for the thrill of shocking someone stopped being funny the first day of school.

Miss Larsen picked us up from the cafeteria, which was not carpeted, as I was showing my friends what my dad drew on my lunch bag. Some kids got sweet little "I love you" notes scrawled on their napkins in cursive. But my dad sketched messages in thick black magic-marker block letters: "Danger: Contains Kool-Aid from Guyana." My lunch bag had gained celebrity status, prompting all the kids to gather around the table to see the day's message. They screamed, "Eww." Then, one kid backed away from the table, cautioning, "I wouldn't eat it." Everybody thought my dad was the coolest, especially me.

"Cute. Who did that?" Miss Larsen, who looked like a blonde Jackie O, asked with her arms crossed over her schoolgirl plaid suit.

"My dad," I beamed back, nearly splitting open with pride.

Besides the principal and vice principal, Miss Larsen was the only other person with an office. A single lamp with a scarf tossed over it cast a shadow against the wall that looked like a grape gumdrop. When she closed the door, Ellie and I stopped and "sprayed" the floor with our invisible boy disinfectant spray to clear out boy germs, then dropped down on the floor. Ellie and I called each other the night before to ensure we'd both wear our wrap skirts. I shoved my Bicentennial red, white, and blue skirt under my legs while Ellie kneeled toward her tape recorder. Miss Larsen settled into her kid-level plastic chair.

"My, what have we here?" she asked as she crossed her legs and inspected our recorders. She probably expected some kind of music.

"We recorded our mothers for you. Wanna hear?" I explained, then clicked my tape recorder on:

Mom: "Get your ass in here now." The sound of a chair screeching across the floor punctuated the command because my mother had shoved me into a chair.

Me: "Ow, damn it."

Mom: "What did you say? Where in the hell did you learn that language?"

(Where in the hell do you think? I glared at her, trying to bore a hole in her head with my eyes.) "Oh, so you think this is funny, you little smart ass? Just for that, I'm going to wash your mouth out with soap." Sounds of water and furious lathering filled the background, then silence as she worked her soapy hands around in my mouth like a dental hygienist.

Me: (Coughing) "Ew."

Mom: "That oughta teach you to keep your damn mouth shut." The sound of a faucet being turned on full blast drowned out the gurgling sound of foam oozing out of my mouth like an overworked horse.

Me: "It's gross."

Mom: The faucet arm gets slammed down with a "ker-chunk." "Did I say you could talk? Children are to be seen and not heard. You got that? When you're 18, you get to speak. But this is my house. My rules. You do as I say." The sound of her footsteps pounding across the orange linoleum floor masked the sound of me spitting the soap down my zippered turtleneck.

Mom: "Matt, get these shoes off the floor now, buster. And who left this glass in the sink? What do I look like? Your God…damn…maid?" Next the sound of a slap, a brief silence, then the sound of Matt crying. Before he could suck in more air for a louder wail, Miss Larsen pushed stop.

Miss Larsen's face looked as pale as the chalk cloud that puffs out when you clap erasers together. Before she could say anything, Ellie's eyes sparkled like mint disks as she punched her play button:

Ellie's mom: "No, you can't have tha- wha-ever thing. What do you think this is? I oughta beat your ass just for asking. You think we're rich?" Next came the sound of a gulp, a glass being set down too hard, and a quick splash.

Ellie: "But Mom, everyone at school has one."

Ellie's mom: "I don't care," her mother slurred the words so it sounded more like, "I own't hair." The sound of a chair skidding across the floor quickly was followed by breaking glass. Ellie's mother was coming after her.

Ellie: "Ouch, you're pulling my hair, Mom!" Ellie screamed so loud, the tape recorder vibrated.

Miss Larsen lunged forward to punch stop, making her blonde hair sway forward like a stage curtain. The End. The green flecks on her suit heaved up and down as she tried to catch her breath. Ellie sat cross-legged on the floor looking up at her with a "What'd ya think" expression illuminating her freckled-splattered face. She seemed to be waiting in anxious anticipation to be told her mother was worse in content than my mother, since my mother always won in the volume department.

"Are you sure I can't call your mothers in here for a conference? It will help you. I promise. Please let me call your mothers," Miss Larsen pleaded pressing her hands down into her legs for emphasis.

"No," we both protested in a panic, but deep down, sadness welled up. I really wanted to understand what I did to make my mother so mad at me all the time.

"She'll kill me. I'm not kidding," I whined because I really was terrified she would kill me.

"My mother would kill me, too," Ellie scampered backwards away from her tape recorder like a crab.

"Well, let's play a game then." With her eyes glaring straight ahead like she'd seen a ghost, Miss Larsen slid Candy Land over to us. In the hierarchy of games, I considered Candy Land the babiest and preferred the heart-pounding suspense of Operation. "So why was your mother so mad, Ellie?"

"I want a new slant-ring binder," Ellie answered. "Everybody has one." It was true, in order to avoid being made fun of, you had to have one as much as Sears Toughskin jeans were an unofficial requirement. The last thing any kid wanted was to be different. Two Turkish kids who wore loopy hand-knitted sweaters and polyester pants paid dearly, never getting picked for dodge ball and receiving a daily deposit of mud-dipped frogs in their plastic homeroom bins.

"Why would that make her so upset?" Miss Larsen cleverly pressed on as we haphazardly pushed the plastic gingerbread men around. Ellie shrugged. "What about you, Jackie, why was your mother so upset? Because you said a bad word?"

"No, she's always like that." My mother raged at me no matter what I did, whether I drew on a wall or brought home a complimentary note from school. She might have liked me better if I were a vending machine that dispensed free

Pepsi and cigarettes, her two favorite things.

"She put soap in your mouth?" Miss Larsen acted so surprised, but I thought everyone's parents took the expression "wash your mouth out with soap" literally.

"Yeah, but she usually uses hot pepper." Miss Larsen's shoulders sunk down in defeat, then the bell rang. Ellie and I skipped out to our open space hallway on the way to Social Studies as a school girl defense mechanism kicked in, making our emotions ricochet from the fear of our mothers finding out we exposed their true personalities to the joys of completely terrifying an adult.

As we reached our class and slowed down, I leaned over to Ellie, "We scared Miss Larsen."

"We're spies," Ellie grinned. "It's our secret."

Later, when I heard Ellie's mother chased her down the street with a knife after we moved to a different neighborhood, my heart sank. Our spying wasn't a game anymore. The war with our mothers was real, and Ellie almost lost. I wondered if Ellie told Miss Larsen.

> "Sexual harassment is a sign...
> That they're really not trying to fire me."

5 . OPEN MIC NIGHT

The small bar at Will Baty's Comedy Club hummed quietly like a ship at dock while the big room sat dark. Freshly scrubbed counters waiting to be leaned on, shined. The lazy lap of slow jazz echoed against the walls. The bar sat idle with its honey-stained panels as visible as a wood hull. Soon the club's motor would gurgle into gear when the comics arrived. "The List," the sheet set out for comics to sign up to perform, sat on the bar near the soda fountain power sprayer. Drops of carbonated water left fat bubbles in the paper. I signed around them, making my name into a bridge. I was the first comic to show up for Open Mic Night, so I sat down and studied my jokes while trying to shove the day's events at Muffler International out of my mind.

The morning after comedy graduation, I had dragged myself into my carpet-covered cubicle and discovered a cassette tape recording of my stand-up routine on my desk with the words: "You rocked!" in Helen's handwriting. Helen was the only person in the company who dared to watch my comedy graduation the night before. Everyone else kept any desire apart from working there quiet for fear of being fired. As Helen walked over and congratulated me, my boss Rick came in, hands jingling change in his pockets with that heart-stopping question: "Can I see you for a minute?" I followed him into his office, the real kind with a door and windows, not a box like mine.

"You didn't do any jokes about working here, did you?" he asked nervously. "Because if you did, you know you'll get fired."

"Wow, who told you to say that?" I said flatly. Rick was a quiet guy who bowed to upper level management's every whim all week, then screamed around on a Harley on the weekends.

"Now Jacki," he dropped his head sideways in a mock warning, then slid his chair up to his desk and leaned toward me, "Well, how was it?" I had to stuff the urge to spurt out, Way better than working here, pal. But staying in line with the "problems are opportunities" company motto, I sweetened my response to, "It was an amazing experience." After his "warning," I went back to my computer and pounded out a whole set about working there.

While Muffler International Headquarters was clearly the wrong place for me, the money I made there gave me a tidy appearance of having it all together. I drove a new car and lived without ten roommates while my friends worked at the hottest ad agencies in town and got paid next to nothing. A lot of my friends lost even the worst paying jobs in the recession. But the fact that my company hadn't lost money since the Model T came out made my job relatively safe.

If I could have dissected my work situation at the time, it would have been face-slapping obvious. On one level, I desperately tried to gain my father's approval. Every day, he put on a Jos. A. Bank's suit. So did I. He carried a Cross pen and pencil set. So did I. He toted a Coach briefcase. So did I. On a deeper level, the truth was that I had no idea who I was, so I dropped into what I thought I was supposed to do instead of doing what I wanted to do. Working in corporate was no different than cartwheeling in front of him like a circus monkey on the lawn just dying for either a laugh, or even better, an encouraging word. Comedy shined a spotlight on everything wrong with me, starting with my identity and the fact I was trying to please my dad and not myself.

It's no wonder I wanted to make him proud. He was the one who bought me my first Coach briefcase, gold Cross pen set, and Jos. Bank suit, not to mention drove me and my milk crates filled with sorority trinkets and clothes from Baltimore all the way to Atlanta. After he set up my first's month rent and utilities to get me started, he looked at me one more time and said, "You gotta know this is hard for a father." Tears streamed down his face and mine as he walked down the apartment stairs to his car. I realized we were leaving each other and heading into separate lives for good the minute I heard the car start. The Eberstarker tradition called for following the departing family member wherever they were going - down the street, to the bus stop, or down the jetway, waving furiously. For the first time, I stayed back, half expecting my dad to come back up to my apartment for one last wave. But he was gone, and I was completely alone in a new city, just like I wanted. That's when I felt the gravity of my decision: It was all up to me whether I made it in my own life or not.

Just a few years later, there I was again, ready to take another risk with comedy and waiting for it to blast me away from the corporate track and into stardom, just like I had expected Atlanta to blast me away from college and into a successful adulthood. But I was worried my dad would think less of me if I quit my "real" job to pursue comedy. He could tolerate a lot of things, but not job irresponsibility. Once, I got a job as a server at Huntington Downs Catering Company wearing a puffy low-cut blouse, and straight brown skirt, looking like a little colonial tart. After my shift, I stood around eating leftover miniature quiches with another employee dressed in knickers and buckle shoes, making fun of how even a Revolutionary War hussy wouldn't wear that uniform. He was the owner's son. So that was my first and last day at Huntington Downs Catering. When my dad found out, he was as mad at me as the time I bounced a check. As long as I pursued comedy while gainfully employed, my dad would probably approve.

As soon as 5:30 hit, I bolted out of my cube and headed back on my way to the New Jacki. As I headed to the bathroom carrying a garment bag, the Muffler International executive men popped their heads out of their cubes like gophers, jeering, "Hey, you going on David Letterman tonight? Ha, ha, ha." "Look out, it's Jacki Leno." As I crossed through the glass tube that funneled executives from one building to another like a corporate Habitrail, my blood pressure surged. I kicked the bathroom door open, then shed my navy jacket, ripped the seashell hair band out of my hair, ripped holes in my panty hose, and threw them in the trash. Once I had my black t-shirt, vintage jacket, and jeans on, I spiked my bangs up like a frozen wave, bolted to my car, and raced out of the parking lot. The "interview process" for my new comedy career couldn't start fast enough.

Unless you're Jerry Seinfeld, performing five-minute sets to audition for the club manager at open mic nights is the only way to score paying gigs. The competition to get hired was intense. At the time, four "A" clubs operated in Atlanta, bringing in "A-list" comics off the circuit. If the club liked you, they'd pick you over and over again to go on at their next 25 Open Mic Nights until they thought you were ready to perform. If they really liked you, they'd hire you to start at the bottom as an emcee for actual money. Or, more likely, chicken wings. But Will Baty's Club was different.

Will Baty eagerly put new talent on stage and paid $20. A veteran stand-up comic who had made it to the national scene like our comedy teacher, Will headlined every show himself and selected new talent to appear with him on stage over the weekend. At first, I thought he was a generous guy who must have been so confident of his talent that he shared the stage with new comics. But after hearing a few stories about his shows from our teacher Dave, I realized Will was actually leveraging the stammering inexperience of new comics to make his act look even better.

While the inexperienced comics eagerly delivered their sets, Will sat behind them wearing an Chewbacca mask and furry glove, then picked his Wookiee nose with his shaggy finger, making the audience howl. His timing was so impeccable, the new comic incorrectly thought the laughs were his. That story made me want to avoid auditioning for Will at all, but all I had to do was think of men gawking at me every day at Muffler International to get that "nothing will stop me" feeling right back.

"Here for Open Mic?" When I looked up and saw it was Will, I almost jumped out of my seat. "Want a Coke?"

"Sure," I said. He could have offered me slug juice and I would have said okay.

"Just graduated from Dave's school, huh?" he pulled at his baggy pants and put his foot up on the chair across from me.

"It's that obvious?" I smiled up at him.

"Dave said he sent you guys over. Well, good luck. You'll do great." He winked, plunked down a Coke in a glass so skinny, it looked like it would cough the ice cubes out, and went back behind the bar. Within a half hour, Will Baty's bar crawled with no customers and all comics, the worst "audience" you could ever have. If you could make a comic laugh, then you had yourself a viable joke.

Sass Mouth

When my comedy school friends Dan, Sarah, and Phil showed up and pulled a bunch of round cocktail tables together, I breathed a sigh of relief. At least we would laugh for each other. When Dan sat down, his Hawaiian shirt sat around him like a tiki hut. Cindy and I looked like comedy twins with our black t-shirt, jeans, and jackets, except gorgeous is a word you could use to accurately describe Cindy. With golden spiral hair, tight aerobic body, and a voice more fragile than Bambi's, her jokes about not being able to get dates made me nervous. No one in their right mind would believe that, but people laughed anyway.

While we sat around glowing about our comedy class graduation the night before, a group of brooding fatigue-clad comics gathered outside smoking with their backs pressed up against the wall. The way they eyeballed us and laughed, I thought they were planning to roll us for our nachos. Dave warned us about them. They were rogue comedians who despised anyone who took Dave's class and were known to carry cans of deviled ham in their military-style coats to use as props in their sets. Their mission: Drive the new comics away, minimize the competition, and secure their rightful places on every list in town.

Will jumped up on the "stage," a rectangular-shaped platform with a lone microphone. With wild eyes that bulged out like goldfish and wiry silver hair, Will could score laughs eating toast. He was letting everyone go on stage, instead of picking just a few like the other clubs do. We were the show and the audience. "Great to see everybody. You know the drill. Do five minutes. If you're good, I'll pay you $20 to do your set this Saturday night. Okay, first up. Jacki Eberstarker? What the hell kind of name is that? Come on up." The rogue comics laughed a little too hard at that one. Will jumped off stage and walked toward the bar.

I climbed up on stage, but when I tried to adjust the microphone, it drooped over, looking phallic. "Uh, Will," I said craning my head under the dangling microphone. "Is there something we should know about you?" Even the rogue comics busted out laughing as Will spun around, tossed his hair around like salad, ran back to the stage, and frantically adjusted the microphone.

Then, I made the biggest mistake ever and started my set with: "So I just graduated from comedy school." The rogue comics immediately launched into a booing frenzy. But I kept going with the same set I did at graduation despite their jabs. Since Dave infused a dash of pity into his introductions at comedy graduation, my first open mic night was a true test. There was no cigarette fog to hide behind. No pity-infused "Be kind, this is her first time on stage" introductions. The "stage" wasn't high off the ground, so I could see every person and hear every ice cube struggling to surface in the too-small glasses.

The rogue comics leaned back in their chairs, completely jaded. My comedy class friends leaned forward, smiling and anticipating every word. As I delivered each joke, my jaw felt as wooden as a nutcracker's. But when I launched into my self-deprecating jokes, even the rogue comics couldn't help but laugh. So I loosened up and tried out some new material.

"My mother was a cop; my father was an insurance man. So people were always saying, 'Oh, so that's if your mother got shot, you'd have insurance?'" Dead silence, punctuated by a few charitable claps from my comedy class friends. "Actually, my father already filled out the claim form...on their wedding night." Moans, no laughs followed this now-dead set with a few, "Oh, man. That's cold." So I stepped it up with my bra jokes and recovered, ending with a good laugh with my Catholic school joke.

Each of the rogue comics added, "Hi, I'm Jacki, and I just graduated from comedy school" to their sets. At the end of the show, Will came back on stage and said: "You all did great. But I have to say, the newest comic wins, and it's Jacki Eber-creeker. Let's give a big hand to Jacki Bleeker. See you Saturday night, Jacki."

One rogue comic slammed his can of deviled ham down on the table with a "Damn it." I'm not sure if any of the rogue comics had day jobs, but I was certain they really needed that $20. I wondered if I would end up like them one day – bitter, broke, and ham-less. Almost everyone in my comedy class cheered, except Phil. "Why her?" he yelled out. "Because she was funny," Will shot back over his shoulder as he walked back to the bar. I got the feeling he and his Chewbacca finger had special plans for me.

When I got home after scoring my first paying gig, Trixie cheered so loud, the neighbors upstairs hammered at the floor with a broom for us to shut up.

"See, I told ya, Eberstarker. This is what you're supposed to do, not mufflers or whatever the hell it is you do," she said while lifting a sculpture of a male torso she had just picked up from her pottery class. "You like?" she said, pointing to his anatomically correct and quite attractive penis.

"Well, it's as close to the real thing as I've gotten for awhile," I said.

When Trixie's mother visited, she'd object: "Oh Trixie!" seeing all the naked sculpted male torsos around the apartment. One time, I put boxers on all of them. "Oh yeah, your mother will love this one," I said as Trixie ignored me.

"Damn it, Eberstarker," Trixie turned around with her hands on her hips. "Comedy is what you're supposed to do, man. Now go call your dad."

"You're a professional now," he said, making me giddy for days. "That's really great, hon." I could feel his excitement through the phone. When I hung up, Trixie stood at my door with her hair all twisted up and a full-length t-shirt painted to look like she was wearing a bikini. "Alright, Little Missy. You're gonna need some cool clothes and makeup, for God's sake." She swore I never wore makeup. I did, just in "natural," barely there hues. Being seen in The South without makeup was as shocking to people as Jesus appearing in a forkful of spaghetti on a billboard. I listened to Trixie and took myself to the mall that weekend, purchasing a hot pink t-shirt, vest with glittery beads and black jeans. Add a bunny, and I could have passed for a magician.

The night of my first paid gig at Will Baty's, I arrived early and sat at the bar.

"Look at you," he said, pulling a bar stool up next to me. "That'll look great on stage. You know, you're a very pretty girl." I choked on my ice cubes. "But you don't think you're pretty, do you?"

"Uh. No," I said, shocked by the use of the word "pretty."

"Well, what about boyfriends?" he asked with his goldfish eyes widening.

"Don't have one. Don't want one," I said. After two disastrous relationships in a row, I was on a self-imposed dating hiatus. Comedy was my boyfriend now.

"Aw, come on. You have natural beauty, don't have to wear a lot of makeup, nice body, and smart as hell. What more could a guy want?"

"You're full of it," I said, smiling at the makeup comment, since he would agree with Trixie for sure.

"You'll do great tonight," he punched me in the arm as he hopped off his stool and headed to the stage.

Behind me, a crowd of customers stood in line at the ticket window. Dressed more for a play than a comedy show, the customers seemed much older than the typical comedy crowd. Will called me into the stage area, which was à la Carson, Leno, and Letterman with a live band on one side, a sofa, and a desk. There wasn't a Green Room per se, just a spot near the bread warmer in the kitchen. Terror pulsed through my veins as the show started, making the skin under my vest sprout sweat, so I got out the set I scrawled on a piece of paper and studied it as waiters barked orders to the chef behind me.

The show moved along with comedy bits in between music sets and Will interviewed tonight's guests, a professional wrestler and his wife, a professional stripper. The crowd constantly roared at Will. Suddenly, they quieted politely as he gave me a gracious introduction and called me to the stage.

"You know how some people have an aura? My aura is blue...as in Blue Light Special," I leaned into the microphone. "Because I attract every loser in a 50-mile radius."

"Last week, this guy picks me up and says, 'Mind if we stop at an ATM machine?' So I said, 'Sure,' and he goes, 'Where's your bank?'"

"This one guy sent me flowers. The card read: 'Just because...I'm stalking you.'"

Just as the audience burst out laughing, I turned around to see what Will was doing, but he was just sitting there, listening. No Chewbacca mask. No antics. His eyes bulged out in mock surprise, and he popped straight up in his seat, making the audience laugh harder. We made a peek-a-boo game out of it, and the audience loved it. I moved into my clown set and bra jokes, looking over my shoulder nervously. But still, no Wookiee finger. Will was on his best behavior, and the audience still loved him even when he was sitting still. So I decided to try a new joke I added to my set at the last minute.

"I still can't believe my father and mother actually procreated. I think my father said, 'Okay, okay I'll do it, but you've gotta wear this bag over your head.'" Groans. I not only lost them, they started hating me. That was the second time mother jokes had bombed, prompting me to add two more comedy rules to my list: In The South, the mother is an institution. Don't make fun of any mother in The South.

Turning to the safety of my bra jokes gave me the big finish I needed. In the Johnny Carson/David Letterman style, Will called me over to the couch, as the wrestler and stripper couple shook my hand and scooted over.

"Tell everybody what you do for a living," Will said.

"I work in mufflers," I said flatly, making the crowd roar.

After the show, people in the audience made it a point to congratulate me. Two women with hair stacked to the ceiling walked over to me. "Honey," one said in a raging New York accent. "Don't make fun of your mutah."

"Yeah, don't make fun of your mutah," the other woman echoed in a voice scarred by cigarettes.

"I can see right through you. Right from the audience. You get yourself a nice therapist, sweetheart," she said, as my heart sank.

"That's right, you've got issues, it's obvious," the other woman said. "And you're so cute," she said, patting me on the cheeks with both hands that smelled of rose-scented lotion. "You'll get yourself straightened out. You'll see."

Just then, a man that looked like Frankie Valli with a turtleneck and slim cigarette pants bounded over to me, I hoped, to tell me how great I was. "Congratulations," he said with a wide grin. "You are the first female loser comic I've ever seen." I stifled the urge to run. "No really," he said giddily. "You've got something here. No one else is doing girl loser." A priceless lamp crashed over in my mind. Suddenly, I felt trapped in a vacuum between wanting to burst into tears and confusion so dense, I could barely move. As I stood there wondering, but wait, *Does that mean I'm a loser?*, candles flickered out on empty tables, and the audience filed out.

> *"When I grew up, I was popular...*
> *With my imaginary friends."*

6 . TWINKLE, TWINKLE LITTLE CHILD STAR

Halfway through sixth grade at Colonial Elementary School, Dad transferred to a new office, so my parents built their dream house in Millwood, closer to his work. Moving from Happy Valley to Millwood marked the pinnacle of a steady climb from blue collars to white ruffled ones by Ralph Lauren. On moving day, we piled into Ironside, headed past the split-levels, ranches, and colonials of Happy Valley for the last time, and jetted onto the highway like a rocket-propelled log.

Forty minutes later, Ironside rolled through a sea of private schools with lacrosse fields, clapboard houses converted into upscale shops, and golf courses spread out like blankets. The engine roared as Ironside headed up a vertical hill, then stammered at the top as if the climb were too ambitious, and we were about to roll right back down to Happy Valley where we belonged. With a metallic whine, Ironside lunged and deposited us at the top, then sighed as the road leveled out and we picked up speed.

"This is nothing like Happy Valley," I said as my anger of being ripped out of sixth grade at Colonial Elementary dampened my parents' controlled giddiness. Millwood was nothing like the modest row houses my dad grew up in where people grew tomato plants in tiny patches of soil and barely had enough grass to justify mowing. In the working class neighborhood where my mother grew up, people rented out half their houses when times got tough. It was no wonder they were excited to move to Millwood and no surprise my protests annoyed them. I'm sure they thought that moving to a nicer neighborhood was the best thing for the whole family.

"Shut the hell up. You haven't even seen it yet," my mother snapped, then took a long drag on her cigarette and blew a line of smoke out the window dreamily. I've seen enough to know I hate it already, I said to myself to avoid being tossed out the tailgate.

Unlike Millwood, Happy Valley provided a level playing field. The houses were identical. Everyone drove American-made cars and wore clothes void of brand names. The sidewalks curled around the development like one long ribbon, making it easy for kids to ride bikes to each other's houses effortlessly. But Millwood was curvy and unpredictable with private driveways tucked away at every turn and no sidewalks for bikes. When Dad proudly pointed out the Mercedes, BMWs, and Porsches as they screamed past us going fifty miles an hour, my stomach sank. We weren't going to fit in Millwood any more than Ironside would shine at an exotic car show.

We hit a straightaway, then rolled to a stop before ramping up a road with no street sign. Our private road, shared with four other custom-built houses. Our stately two-story brick colonial stood proudly in a freshly flattened square of land. Woods wrapped around the house like a rich lady wearing a mink stole. Another two-story brick colonial was still under construction next door, which meant no kids to play with. My throat squeezed, trying to choke back my protests that there was nothing there for us – no candy store, no pool, no friends. I wanted to throw a rock at it and run right back to Happy Valley, but my father pulled me inside.

The kitchen smelled like a chemical spill. A woman with a chestnut-colored beehive hair-do wearing a cleaning smock spread a stinky blob of pink foam on the built-in range. When she saw me, she lit up. "Aw hon, you're the luckiest little girl in Bal-more."

"Me? Why?" I sulked, as my brothers raced up the stairs to claim their rooms.

"Don't you know you have a movie star living behind you?" she said, eyes wide in mock delight. The words "movie star" stopped me cold. Names buzzed through my head: Lindsay Wagner from *Bionic Woman*? Farah Fawcett? Or with my luck, the bratty Veruca Salt from *Willy Wonka & the Chocolate Factory*?

"Who?" I said.

"She's a little girl about your age. She just moved here from California. Oh,

I'm sure she'd love to have a friend like you." Score, I thought.

"Would you hand me dat wudder bottle, hon," she asked me, speaking classic Baltimoron and motioning to a spray bottle on the counter. In the Baltimoron language, the "T" has mysteriously disappeared from the words Baltimore and water.

"But who is she?" I said, still dazed.

"Her name is Leigh Benton. She's the school teacher's daughter's best friend on *The Pioneers*," she beamed. I had no idea who she was. Actually, her star status required explanation since she wasn't an easily recognizable "star" of the show. Soon I'd find out that most children recognized her as the "star" of "Recess," a made-for-TV movie about a girl and her ailing horse named Recess. Kids also knew her as the little girl dancing with a giant bunny in a "Bun Buns" cereal commercial. When they saw her, kids sang: "Bun Buns are fun funs!" The fact that I had no idea who she was didn't matter to me. She could have visited a Hollywood set, and I would have been impressed. Having a friend was all I wanted, but having a movie star friend exceeded my brain capacity. I stared into the woods, searching for the movie star.

"It's dat house right dere, hon," the cleaning lady said, pointing to a house that looked like an English cottage on steroids. I want to see her right now, I thought, then charged up to my room to get a better look.

To my delight, the back window in my room offered a clear view of her house. As soon as it got dark, I shut off my lights, stretched out on my bed like a lizard, and kept my eyes trained on her window hoping to see her. Shaped like a movie screen, her bedroom window supplied me with front row seats. This fact alone made the move from Happy Valley to Millwood suddenly worth it. Just as I started to give up on seeing her, there she was, darting around her room, probably getting ready for a show. Why was she here in Millwood and not Hollywood? I wanted to be her friend so badly, but I was too terrified to go down there. I knew I wasn't cool enough to be her friend. So, I did the safe thing and spied on her.

Sometimes, she carried a steaming mug into her room, carefully maneuvering around her sofa, roll-top desk, and huge bed as if she were navigating a tight rope. Her room was as twice as big as mine with her own phone and stereo. Once, she talked on the phone for almost two hours, a feat that would earn me a police-mother beating for sure. Then one night, she stared right back at me. My body cemented itself into a mold, rolled off the bed, and dropped to the floor like a statue. "What the hell's going on up there," my mother screeched up the stairs. Leigh's curtains stayed closed all fall. That's when I realized the only way to meet her was to just go down there, and quit being such a sissy.

After school the next day, I played what the lady with the beehive said over and over in my mind: "I'm sure she'd love to have a friend like you." Then, I got up the courage to go down there. I tiptoed through the overgrown trail that snaked through the woods from our house to hers. The sticker bushes poked through my jeans, and rain popped the leaves around me. When I rounded the corner to the front of her house, I stopped dead. There she was up close, sitting in a cube of a window, leaning back in a leather chair and talking on the phone. When I tapped the brass doorknocker, she swung her black leather Scandinavian chair around so the back blocked me from seeing her.

A very Hansel and Gretel door with a small iron-framed window and latch door hardware creaked open. "Yes?" a woman glared at me with charcoal eyeliner rimming her eyes and silver wisps spiraling through her black hair like wire. I assumed she was Leigh's mother.

"Hi, my name is Jackie. I live in the house behind you and wanted to see if I could, well, meet your daughter?" I am such a geek, my toes curled into my shoes. After watching an episode of *The Pioneers*, I tried to learn as much as I could about Leigh's character so I wouldn't embarrass myself, but I did anyway. Leigh had a minor recurring role that required real acting ability, like bursting into tears and reacting to a tragic farm accident, but nothing I could discuss with her mother intelligently.

"I'm not a fan, " I explained to her mother. Way to go, that's like saying you don't like her daughter. "I just want to be friends." Because I don't have any.

"Just a minute," she said. She left the door cracked and whispered to Leigh.

"But Mom, I'm talk-ing to Kay-la," Leigh yelled, pronouncing mom with a W. Hearing her scream at her mother like that made me cringe, expecting her mother to slap her. But her mother didn't say anything. With one well-manicured hand, Mrs. Benton pulled the door open and looked at me sternly, as if I had done something wrong. "Leigh's busy. You'll have to come back another time." Then, she shut the door and the doorknocker knocked itself.

As I stood there thinking my mother was right, I was not good enough to even talk to Leigh Benton, an internal rage ignited a fire under my skin. I am never going to have any friends here. I pounded back through the path and this time, I didn't care about the stickers stabbing my legs. When I got home, my mother sat Indian-legged on the sofa eating corn flakes out of a glass measuring cup. "What the hell's your problem? Couldn't find any friends?" she smirked. At least I try to have friends. To my knowledge, my mother didn't have any friends. Eventually, she'd campaign to win neighborhood friendships by doing whatever it took, from driving them to appointments to scrubbing their floors after parties.

Leigh's private driveway dipped down off of Bridlepath Way, a street full of other custom-built houses and private school kids. The way the Bridlepath people reacted to everyone on our private drive, you'd think our houses blocked their ocean view. We weren't invited to their crab feasts, got left out of their neighborhood directory, and barely got acknowledged when we saw them at the store. But I was so desperate to have someone to play with, I turned my attention to the Bridlepath kids anyway. I quickly found out they played with me sparingly, as if I were a rabid raccoon.

My first time playing at Allison Frishy's house turned out to be my last when her mother warned her a girl named Morgan was "almost here, honey." They exchanged a look that said our play date was a limited time offer. Allison jumped up, kicked over her model horse and miniature fence, and informed me it was time for me to leave. Now. Morgan was coming over. I wondered why I wasn't good enough to play with them. My lack of brand-name clothes and private school stature probably had a lot to do with it. Maybe my tennis shoes and jeans just screamed "Common" a little too loudly. Or maybe her mother worried she wouldn't get invited to join the Junior League if Allison were caught playing with the Public School Girl.

Although the private school parents seemed to endorse their children's exclusive private-school-only behavior, they didn't hesitate to use me to babysit their little ones. Since their lives appeared so rich on the outside, I expected abundance on the inside. But when I babysat, I discovered the inside of their lives were as hollow as a chocolate Easter rabbit. While they adorned their kids with Izod labels and drove Mercedes station wagons, their cabinets were bare. Although I had no idea what nouveau riche meant at the time, my education had begun, fueling my lifelong suspicion that ostentatious people wielded possessions to compensate for lack of character.

Deciding that I would never be like them didn't seem to matter. Living in Millwood made my emotions dart back and forth like a nervous fish from self-pity to pure rage. I slumped home from Allison's house feeling sorry for myself that I wasn't good enough to get invited to play, too. One minute, I knew they were right, telling myself: No one likes me. I am a stupid loser— all facts confirmed by my mother's calling me "stupid bitch" every day. Then on a good day, the rage filled me with new hope: I'll show those preppy snoblets one day. I'll make my own way in this world. I don't need them. They'll see.

Kicking through the charred leaves back through the trail in the woods from Allison's house to mine, I suddenly heard an acoustic guitar playing Led Zeppelin outside. I walked toward the sound and discovered a guy sitting on the bumper of his car at the house next to ours. His head down, he expertly played a honey-colored guitar with stripes through it like molasses. When a branch snapped under my shoe, he stopped and looked right at me. With sandy blonde hair and crystal blue eyes, he reminded me of Luke Skywalker. Seeing him was like the sensation of chewing Freshen-Up Gum for the first time and getting that unsuspected squirt from the hidden mint gel in the middle. Something had changed in me; gum chewing would never be the same.

"Hey there, are you my neighbor?" he asked. His blonde hair fanned back as he flipped his guitar neck down to the ground.

"Yeah, I think so," I answered as my feet suddenly slid out from under me, down a mound of wet grass onto the asphalt. Instead of landing on my butt, I nailed the landing with both feet. All of that practice sticking landings in gymnastics was worth it to save embarrassment in front of my first love.

"I'm Dave Grayson," he said, uncrossing his legs and leaning forward to shake my hand.

"I'm Jackie Eberstarker," I said, hoping he couldn't hear the "and I love you" end of the sentence sounding off inside my prepubescent head.

"Eber what?" he said, leaning over closer as if he didn't hear me.

"Starker. Everyone laughs at our name. Sometimes they call us Eberstreaker." When he laughed, his thick eyelashes almost made a straight line. He was blessed with the kind of eyelashes women swoon over because they would never require mascara.

"So you're the all-American family next door? I've seen you all dressed up going to church," he said.

"Church? Maybe Peppy's Pizza." He laughed harder this time. At the last Catholic mass we went to, two guys with beards, canvas ponchos, and leather sandals sang "holy, holy, holy" while shaking tambourines and furiously strumming their guitars. I thought it was a reenactment of a Jesus scene. "But I thought he was a carpenter," I whispered to my dad, who choked on his Tic Tac. "No, they're folk Catholics. You know, hippies," he said as he slid out of the pew for Holy Communion. Dad never questioned why people did things, he just got in line. Dad wasn't Catholic, but he went to Communion because everyone else did. Plus, free snack. That was back when I wore a plaid v-neck pleated jumper and saddle shoes during my short stint as a Private School Girl from kindergarten to third grade.

Our days of church going ended right there because my parents said the church kept demanding too much money. When I asked my mother if I could go to a private school in Millwood, she promptly reminded me that only smart kids got accepted into private schools and that I only got into Catholic school just because I was a card-carrying Catholic. I thought if I went to a private school, I would be assured acceptance and friendship. But my mother's response confirmed that my mission to find friends here was hopeless, until now.

"So, do you like it here?" Dave asked and wedged his orange guitar pick in his mouth to tie his shoe.

"No. The kids on Bridlepath don't like us, so I don't have any friends to play with." My heart plunged when I thought of Happy Valley and how none of my friends ever cut a play date short.

"Aw, they're phony over there anyway," he said, alerting my "cool new word" alarm. I loved collecting words, and had quite a dictionary going, including gems like "dweeb" and "dork-wad."

"What do you mean, 'phony'?"

"They think they're better than everybody. Truth is, my dad makes more money than this whole damn neighborhood, but you'd never know it. The hell with them, they don't like us either." From then on, "phony" was my official word for describing the neighbors. Relief washed over me, realizing I wasn't the only one tossed to the neighborhood "reject" pile. It was the only thing Dave and me had in common. And to me, that was cause enough to get married right then, despite the fact that I was a fledgling elementary school girl and he was a full-fledged adult.

"I do notice when I go over there that they have Polo clothes, but no food," I leaned toward him to share what I thought was the neighborhood secret. Dave tipped his head back to the sky and laughed so hard, he almost fell off his car.

"You're alright, Jackie Eberstarker. You're alright." Even though I had no idea why what I just said was so funny, I stood there smiling nervously, as if I had meant the joke. He slid off the bumper of his car, flipped his guitar around to his back, and gave me a high five. "Come over anytime, okay?"

"Sure," I answered as I surveyed the way his "Bojangles Too" t-shirt hung loosely across his broad muscular shoulders. I can't believe he's talking to me like I'm older. He's being nice to me. Right there, all thoughts about Bridlepath and Leigh "Movie Star" Benton evaporated while my whole being filled up with the desire to be Mrs. Dave Grayson.

Instead of watching Leigh from my back window, I turned my attention to my side window and watched for Dave to zip into his driveway. The way his engine sounded when it started alerted me that he was leaving, and the way it downshifted announced he was home. Nearly every day, I rigged up excuses to go to the Grayson's house, toting cups of sugar over they didn't ask for, their *Wall Street Journal*, even dragging one of their unsuspecting dogs home as if it were lost. Mrs. Grayson was almost always home and must have known my true intentions when she poured me tea and said, "Dear Heart, you come over anytime. Keep me company. Dave will be home soon." Besides my mother's mother, Grandmother Wasser, who took care of me every day when I was little while my mother worked, Mrs. Grayson showed me what having a nice mother could be like.

All three Grayson kids, who lived at home, were much older than we were. Peter was twenty-eight. Helen, twenty-six. And, Dave, nineteen - exactly eight years and seven months older than me. Dave trained to become a graphic designer instead of working for his father's company. To make money while he went through design school, he briefly worked at his father's construction and property company, until one day he saw two workers blowing their noses into a trash bin. Seeing their streams of snot was so disgusting, he said he walked off the job right then and decided to pursue his own career. After he graduated from design school, he landed a plum job as staff designer for a firm in downtown Baltimore.

Mrs. Grayson told me all about Dave as I sat wide-eyed at their table, drinking cup after cup of tea. She told me everyone called him Davey and that he had always been a loner. When he was little, she once watched him play every position of an entire baseball game alone. First, he pitched, then swung his imaginary bat, ran the bases while announcing every play as he ran. He loved being outside helping Mr. Grayson every chance he got, clearing the brush out of the woods, mowing the lawn, and plowing the driveway in the winter. Meanwhile, the other Grayson kids hardly ever ventured outside, unless they were going somewhere. I never saw them help Mr. Grayson with the yard or Mrs. Grayson with dinner.

Helen worked downtown as an event planner, wore only top designer clothes, and drove a British racing green Triumph Spitfire 1500. The one time Helen sauntered outside, Dave made fun of her relentlessly, saying, "Do you have a 'Hair by Sassoon' label on your head, Helen? Wait, let me check." He pretended to search through her strawberry blonde hair, curled under in a tight bob. "Get the hell off me," she spat, swatting his hand and retreating into the house. I stepped aside to allow Helen's anger to skirt by me when she snapped at her mother and brothers. Eventually she became like an older sister to me. When I look back on it, Mrs. G probably did everything she could to boost my self-esteem. I suspect she urged Helen to spend time with me, which made me feel special, until my mother leveled me. Helen took me out to lunch and bought me boxes of truffles, balls of chocolate rolled in sprinkles. We popped them in our mouths and chased them down with Cokes. Sometimes she took me with her to the in salons downtown to get my hair cut. When she ran out of room in her closet, I was the lucky recipient of top-brand designer clothes with price tags still dangling off the cuffs.

Peter, the tallest, looked like Robert Redford with a beard and drove the nicest car in the family. Peter worked long hours with Mr. Grayson at Grayson Properties. For the longest time, I only knew his car, a Porsche 911 convertible that hovered in the garage like a red lacquered space ship just waiting to slice air in half. On the dashboard, rolls of mints sat lined up like rolls of coins. But we never touched the candies or the car, fearing the kind of beating we would have endured touching my father's prized Corvette Stingray under cover in the garage. The only time I saw Peter was when he padded his way downstairs for breakfast. But he never talked to me, just snapped *The Wall Street Journal* open to the stock section, cussed if his stocks weren't doing well, then pitched the paper against the wall. He had repeated that action so many times, their two dogs didn't even look up when the paper smashed the wall like a paper bird.

Months went by before I ever met Mr. Grayson. One Saturday, Mrs. Grayson dragged me upstairs to her closet so she could talk to me while she got dressed to go out for a nice dinner in Little Italy downtown with Mr. Grayson.

"Jesus Christ, Vivi," bellowed Mr. Grayson, an American version of Alfred Hitchcock standing there with a robe wrapped around his big belly, ruddy cheeks, and mouth curled down in a disapproving frown. "Clean up this closet. That eight-foot-long ash tray in your car is cleaner than this hell hole." I tried to apply myself to the wall like wallpaper so he wouldn't notice me. But he just stomped past me while Mrs. Grayson laughed.

Mr. Grayson was like the planet at the core of the family's universe. Everyone revolved around him, holding their place in the world with the gravity he provided. He once joked he was the "Great Provider," since he supplied all the family's cars and pretty much anything they wanted. Once Helen wanted an expensive sports car, but Mr. Grayson vetoed the purchase because he didn't like the car's construction, sending Helen into a fit. Peter wanted a tennis court in the yard, but Mr. Grayson refused. He insisted on living a simple, methodical life – eating the same dinner every night except Saturday when he took Mrs. Grayson out, watching the same shows every night, and drinking the same onion-speared martini, no matter what the occasion.

Even after the Grayson's left for dinner, my brothers and I sat on their sofa and watched the back door swing open while Peter, Dave, and Helen's friends funneled in at all hours. The Grayson's door might as well have been revolving the way everyone came busting through it all the time. Not once was it ever locked. And, no one was required to knock. Everyone was welcome.

Everyone called the Graysons Mr. and Mrs. G, a nickname we quickly adopted. If you walked in during dinner, Mrs. G just plunked down another plate and insisted you eat, too. At our house, no one stopped by for dinner without being invited. If something spilled or one of the dogs pulled a ham off the counter, Mrs. G just laughed, which provided a stark comparison to how my mother reacted when our Old English Sheep dog grabbed a steak off the counter. My mother sprayed him with mace and wrestled him to the ground until she got the steak back. I wondered how some people like Mrs. G could have so much fun in their lives while my mother only had anger.

Watching Mrs. G work in the kitchen was like a lost episode of *I Love Lucy*. Instead of scraping the dishes into the sink and funneling the food down with the disposal, she dumped everything in at once and stopped up the sink. Then, she rolled up her sleeves and plunged her arms through the murky water. Slimy lettuce twisted around like silk in a washing machine and T-bones popped to the surface like bony sharks. Next, she flipped on the disposal, sending a plume of lettuce-filled water exploding out of the sink.

"Geezy preece," she said, sending her hand back in for another dive.

"Why don't you just use the disposal first instead of dumping it all together?" I asked.

"I know, I know," she said, using her free hand to toss Pepperidge Farm cookies to their black lab, Bailey, and Cookie, a mutt that looked like a beagle who swallowed a keg.

Other Grayson relatives called her "Crazy Vivi" for tying Cookie, who was in heat, to a tree and hanging out the back window with a BB gun shooting the ugly suitor-dogs away. Whenever Mrs. G came over, our mother would use her singsongy voice and act all nice, setting out tea, cookies, and an extra-deep ashtray meant for sharing. After multiple afternoons sitting at our kitchen table for hours talking, she became trusted friends with our mother. If one of us walked into the room, my mother would launch into show-off mode and put her ultimate control of her children on display. As she barked orders and insults at us, Mrs. Grayson pleaded with her, "Oh, Pat. Don't talk to those children like that. Those kids are going to hate you, Pat. Oh I wouldn't know what to do if my kids hated me. Aren't you afraid they'll hate you?" Too late, I thought. In response, my mother focused on the ashtray between them, glided her cigarette down for a featherlight landing, tapped the ashes off daintily, and promptly changed the subject.

Anyone else even remotely criticizing my mother's handling of her children earned them a blunt, "Shut the hell up and mind your own business." But Mrs. G was different. My mother ran to her rescue anytime, any place. If Mrs. G needed to go to an appointment, my mother rearranged her schedule to take her. If she needed a prescription in the middle of the night, my mother happily fetched it. If her own children needed anything, my mother exploded at the inconvenience. Friendship and respect from outsiders was clearly something my mother worked hard to earn. But with us, respecting my mother was a requirement, not something that needed to be earned from her children or reciprocated in any way. Mrs. G remained my mother's only neighborhood friend until a freak ice storm hit. Then, she expanded her friendship horizons to the Bridlepath Way.

One winter day, we woke up to an eerily quiet morning. There were no sounds of traffic on the main road. No parents getting ready for work. All night, rain had turned to sleet. In the morning, Millwood was still except for the soft pattering of snowflakes piling up on an ice-encrusted blanket. Because of the treacherous ice, the entire city shut down, leaving us home with our mother and father. Suddenly, the phone rang, and I heard my mother say, "Okay, Carol. We'll be right over." Carol, as in Leigh's mother, Carol Benton. My mother walked back into the living room. "Now's your big chance to meet the movie star," she said, clenching a cigarette with her teeth, squinting from the smoke licking at her eyes, and strapping on snow boots at the same time. "Those damn Bridlepath kids are pranking the Bentons, and I guess *I'm* going to have to handle it. Get your ass in gear, you're coming with me."

We kicked through the snow as it filled in a fat shaving cream S on the path between our house to the Benton's. Mrs. Benton let us through one of the sliding glass doors in the back of the house. Mattie, a nervous weiner dog, bolted through the door with a crunch as her hotdog body crashed through the layer of ice. "Leigh, come get Mattie," Mrs. Benton called over her shoulder, sending a bolt of excitement through me, which quickly faded as I prayed Leigh wouldn't remember all those times she called: "Mattie" and my brothers and I yelled: "What-ee." At Happy Valley, our antics were far worse with the next door neighbor who bellowed: "Ho, ho, ho" to halt his drooling bull dog while we answered: "Merry Christmas."

"Tea?" Mrs. Benton asked with a sense of urgency. Every phone in the house blared and echoed off the hardwood floors like alarms in a fire station. Looking around their living room, I noticed there was not one piece of colonial furniture or mallard duck, a violation of Baltimore decorating code. Scandinavian furniture and wool rugs carefully placed in the center of each room made a clear statement that they were not from around here. Mrs. Benton walked from room to room with her ballet flats making funny click-clicks on the hardwood, then muffled clomp-clomps on the carpet and back.

"They keep screaming: 'Is Leigh home, home on the range?' Then, they hang up," she explained, nervously bobbing a tea bag in a metal Japanese teapot. "They must be jealous of Leigh. They've been calling here all day. This is a business phone." The phones wailed again. Mrs. Benton winced, then shut her eyes.

"Let me answer it," my mother said in her "let the police handle this" tone.

"Fine. Fine," Mrs. Benton shakily stretched the phone cord out of the kitchen and handed her the receiver.

"This is Officer Eberstarker speaking. Let me speak to your parents. Now," she commanded, then her jaw dropped. "Damn it. Those little assholes hung up on me," she said, at first astonished, then self-assured. "Well, that oughtta shut them up for a while." The phone rang again just as Officer Eberstarker returned to her seat, making Mrs. Benton jump as she nervously filled my mother's cup. The way the prank-call situation upset Mrs. Benton, you'd think a madman with a chainsaw was at the front door. But it was just a bunch of lower school kids with nothing better to do. The phones started blaring again when Leigh appeared.

"Hi, I'm Leigh," she seemed bored, with her hands stuffed into the pockets of her lemon-colored corduroy overalls. I shot my mother a *See, she's wearing overalls* look that went ignored. My mother wouldn't let me wear them because she said, "You are not going to run around this neighborhood looking like a God damned farm girl." And here a genuine movie star sported them.

"Hi," I answered, trying to appear cool as if her TV self didn't impress me. A thin strip of gold twisted into the shape of a heart with a tiny gold key dangling next to it hung around her neck. When I asked her where she got it, she fumbled with it and told me Tiffany's. The "had to have" necklace in Millwood was an add-a-bead, a gold chain with a bunch of gold balls. The more balls you had strung across your neck, the cooler you looked. I wanted Leigh's look, special. Different. Hollywood. But when I went to the Jewel Hut at Millwood Mall and asked where Tiffany's was, they laughed, "You've got the wrong mall, hon. You need dat one up 'dere in New York er somethin'."

"Let's go upstairs," Leigh said. When we reached her room, I nearly fainted when I realized you could see everything in our house straight from her movie-screen-shaped window.

"Wow, nice view," I said weakly, wondering if she could see me watching her, even though I turned the lights off.

"Yeah, a great view for some people to stare at me through the window," she said bitterly. Her words felt like a slap. Maybe she was watching me watching her? My legs folded like paper accordions. She hates me. "So do you actually like it here?" she said sarcastically. I felt my chances of being her friend open back up again.

"Hate it," I said, trying to sound cool.

"Are you friends with the Bridlepath kids?"

"Hate them," I said, getting a rhythm going. "They don't like me."

"Oh, Allison Frishy doesn't like you, either?" Leigh said, pushing her pillows around her sofa in front of the window.

"She's such a piggy face," I blurted out, and Leigh threw herself backwards into the pillows, cracking up.

"Oh my God, she does have a piggy face." Being rejected by the Bridlepath kids suddenly had its advantages. Leigh needed a friend, too. Now we were in the same club.

Soon after the prank callers were identified as none other than Allison Frishy and her equally piggy-faced brothers, my mother called up the stairs that it was time to go. Leigh politely asked if I could stay longer, and to my complete surprise, my mother said yes. Somehow Leigh had disarmed my mother. Normally, she flattened anything she thought would make me happy. She knew I wanted to be friends with Leigh. Maybe the thought that her daughter would be playing with a Hollywood star paved the way to yes.

Leigh and I talked for so long, we watched the snow fill up my mother's footsteps on the trail. I learned that Leigh was from California, and California people were ahead on everything, which was one reason Leigh hated Maryland. In California, roller skating disco in the streets was hot, a trend that had never hit Baltimore, due to the high risk of getting mowed down by a speeding car. So Leigh took to rollerskating in the basement listening to Buddy Holly, which I thought was so weird because that was my dad's music. She missed her California friends and roller skating parties while I missed my Happy Valley friends and having friends closer than thirty miles. We had nothing in common and everything in common.

Leigh Benton was once described to me as a forty-year-old trapped in a girl's body. It was no wonder. Her parents treated her as if she were forty. When she acted her real age of thirteen, they dismissed her as if she were a forty-year-old just acting silly. They acted more like roommates than parents and child. Not once did I ever see them sit down with Leigh or hug her. But when they introduced her to their friends, a great sense of pride filled up the room as they announced, "And this...This is Leigh." Everyone stood in awe of the little movie star as she trotted out in her prairie girl skirt, vintage brooch, and cowboy boots. And she met their gazes steadily. Even as a thirteen-year-old, she owned their applause. I longed to be that special and to evoke such pride and admiration from people. But I was just a sniveling wanna-be, barely worthy of taking a job as president of Leigh's fan club. Or, so I thought. At least around me, she was free to act her age.

Hearing Mr. and Mrs. Benton talk to each other was like listening to public television. Eventually, it became obvious to me that they thought I was excessively stupid, once asking me, "You do know how to set a table, don't you?" Then, I dazzled them by pulling the utensil basket straight out of the dishwasher and carrying it across the kitchen instead of walking back and forth five hundred times. "Well, I didn't know you could do that," Mrs. Benton said in amazement. Although it was obvious to me that the Bentons thought I was in no way good enough for their daughter, it became clear that they allowed the friendship because my family provided a convenient babysitting solution for them. The ice storm was the first and last time my mother and Mrs. Benton ever socialized together. From that day on, Leigh shuttled back and forth between houses while the Bentons were out.

Mr. Benton, a corporate attorney, moved closer to his Washington and New York clients so he could entertain them while carving out new business in Baltimore. Meanwhile, Mrs. Benton spent her time raising money for high-profile charitable causes. Between them, they were never home, leaving Leigh to do as she pleased or stay at our house. We stayed at Leigh's house a lot, where she introduced me to beer, pot, and Mr. Dorchester.

> *"I'm still wearing a training bra...*
> *No idea what they're training for."*

7 . BAD JACKIE

Nothing was off-limits to Leigh Benton. As a mere seventh grader, she casually reached into the refrigerator and pulled out two beers – right in front of her father. He walked by her in a tuxedo fumbling with his tie without saying a word while he was getting ready for a black-tie fundraiser that night. The nervous, yet contained, energy vibrated around him like the squiggly-lined cartoons in *The New Yorker*. I numbly followed Leigh and her beers straight upstairs. "Beer is really good for your hair," she announced over her shoulder on the way up to her bathroom, featuring a huge mirror and stage lights around it like a marquee.

She ran the bath water and cracked open a can. "We'll use this one on our hair and drink the other one," she said, tossing me a towel. I leaned my head into the tub and lathered raspberry-scented Suave into my hair. The frigid foam seared into my head as Leigh dumped one can over me, then tipped back the other can. "Here," she said, handing me the can. The bubbles burned the back of my throat, and I caught my breath. I had to be the first kid in sixth grade to consume alcohol. The sensation felt like one billowy jellyfish rising up my throat and trying to surface out the top of my skull. As for the beer-as-hair-product, she was right, my straight hair fell like bunches of silky strands you pull out of corn. But just like on TV, no way would I "try this at home." I'd get arrested.

Ever since Leigh and I met during the blizzard, we'd been inseparable. Whenever Mrs. Benton took Leigh shopping, they brought me along. The Bentons once took me on a road trip up the East Coast, listening as we read *Othello* aloud. Leigh's voice arched high in delight and plunged into dramatic despair, while mine droned as flat as a first grader at a Christmas pageant. Her parents went out nearly every night, leaving Leigh and me free to run back and forth between houses with flashlights. Eventually, no one paid attention to us, not even my mother.

Sometimes on the weekends, Leigh's teachers, Mr. Dorchester and Mr. Santoni, entertained Leigh while her parents went out. Seeing teachers on weekends was about as weird to me as having the name of your school plastered on the back of your car. The Benton's station wagon had a moon roof and Breighton School plastered on the back window so everyone knew exactly what school she went to. Ironside did not have a moon roof or a Hazelwood Elementary School sticker on the back window because nobody cared what public school we went to.

As Leigh fired up her blow dryer, the doorbell rang, and Mrs. Benton called up to us. Just as Mr. Dorchester and Mr. Santoni stepped inside the foyer, Leigh's parents sashayed out the door. Leigh sent me downstairs to tell the teachers she was still drying her hair.

"You must be Bad Jackie," Mr. Dorchester said, bending his former-basketball-star frame over to shake my hand.

"Bad?" I said.

"That's what Leigh calls you – Bad Jackie." I was surprised she called me that. It could have been that sixth grade gambling ring I started in the Hazelwood Elementary cafeteria. Who knew playing Old Maid for money was considered "gambling?" Or that time I got caught passing Judy Blume's *Forever* around the library with all the key sex scenes underlined. But I was even more shocked she even mentioned my name to her teachers – did that mean I qualified as Leigh's real friend? Or was I just the membership director of her non-existent fan club?

Mr. Dorchester's hand felt warm wrapped around mine. His eyes burned hot blue, so intense, they could skewer right through you. "Oh, you didn't know she calls you Bad Jackie?" He smiled, just as quickly, his eyes danced in a flash of turquoise and cobalt. "This is Mr. Santoni."

"Hi," I said, feeling like a timid little mouse standing next to a tall Mr. Dorchester and a medium-height, broad-chested Mr. Santoni. With a mustache that curled up at the ends, he looked like he jumped out of an old-timey boxing poster, dukes up.

"You don't look so bad," Mr. Santoni said, stepping back and jamming his hands in his pockets.

"Jackie, can you come back up here?" Leigh shouted. I charged up the stairs and met a completely dressed Leigh, holding a tin with painted parakeets lined up on a wire on the front. She flicked open the top like a tiny trunk lid, revealing dried up clumps of green dirt. "Let's get high," she said. Too scared to admit I had no idea what that meant, other than listening to Dave Grayson talk about "getting smoked up," I nodded okay. Then my heart raced with excitement – maybe Dave would think I was more grown up if I got high, too. I had already tried wearing silk shorts like Linda Ronstadt and getting a spirally perm like Stevie Nicks to look more adult, but it didn't work. The silk shorts kept giving me wedgies and the spiral perm made the ends of my hair break off, leaving spikes across the top of my head like a broken fence. After taking all those fashion risks, Dave still saw me as a kid. Maybe if I got experience smoking pot, he'd like me because I got high like an adult.

Leigh pressed the crumbly dirt into a glass pipe as if she were packing brown sugar into a measuring cup. Then she grabbed a lighter out of her roll-top desk and shut the light off. She sat on her sofa and cranked the window, making it swivel like the revolving glass door at Madison's department store. Amazed at my courage, I leaned near the window with her and shoved any fear of Officer Eberstarker seeing us from my mind. In some weird way, I almost wanted her to see us so I could smoke pot and give her the finger simultaneously. As Leigh inhaled, the clump glowed like a hot coal. She held her breath, then pressed her lips against the screen, and blew the smoke outside. Tiny criss-crosses indented her lips. I copied her every move. Inhale. Hold. Blow. But instead of inhaling smoothly, I burned my throat and coughed so hard, I thought my eyes would pop out like marbles. Aborting the mission made smoke snake lazily through her room. "Sorry," I said.

"My parents never come in here anyway," she said.

By the time we got back downstairs, Mr. Dorchester and Mr. Santoni were leaned back in the conversation pit talking. Then they noticed Leigh's eyes, dilated like a raccoon's at night. They shot each other a look. They know. Leigh traced her finger across their backs and circled around to face them. Their eyes stayed fixed on her; they never noticed me. Whenever I was with Leigh, moments like this one served to remind me I was more of an official sidekick than an actual friend. Leigh was always the star, not me. Maybe she hung out with me because my dullness made her star shine even brighter. She once read me an elaborate poem about a eucalyptus tree wrapping its medicinal leaves around a child, then told me she wrote it. My awe in her amazing talent must have amused her before my age-appropriate stupidity eventually bored her.

We all climbed into Mr. Dorchester's Audi station wagon. Leigh called both men by their first names, Paul and Bill. On the way to Pizza Hut, Paul blared Boston's "More Than a Feeling," while Leigh stood on her head in the back seat and flailed around like a fish doing gymnastics, making both of them laugh. I loved it when Leigh acted like a girl and not a frustrated woman trapped inside a girl's body. She was a lot more fun. Making her return to girlhood was my mission. Occasionally, everyone laughed at something I said, then looked at each other in amazement, like they couldn't believe a smart comment came from the public school girl. I watched in awe as Leigh danced around and captivated Paul and Bill and wondered what it felt like to have people think you're so special, they just can't keep their eyes off of you.

After they dropped us off at Leigh's, we collapsed on her sofa and she told me all about the camping trips she'd taken with Mr. Dorchester and Santoni. Each year, they took groups of kids on overnight camping trips along the Appalachian Trail. After they'd hike all day, they'd set up their tents while the teachers started a campfire. That was when all the action happened. While the chaperones were busy getting the fire going, the kids ducked into their tents and drank. During one trip, Leigh watched as her dream boyfriend Heath disappeared into the woods with Stacey and a bottle of scotch Heath stole from his parents. Pretending not to care, she sat around the fire with Paul and Bill and gave them each "back rubs" and "front rubs." I didn't believe her. But the last thing I wanted her to do was to stop telling me about it, so I didn't say anything until she started talking about how she slept in Paul's tent.

"No way," I finally screamed, burying my head in a pillow.

"Way," she said back. "He rolled over and whispered his wife's name in my ear."

"You are so lying," I said, more seriously.

"Hey, you don't have to believe me if you don't want to." She started to get up.

"Wait, why were you in his tent?"

"It's like this. I want Heath. Heath loves Stacey, who has colossal boobs. I'm flat. So I hang around Paul because he loves me. Get it?"

"So Heath will get jealous?"

"Right."

"Does it work?"

"Of course not. Stacey has epic tits."

"Oh."

The reality of Leigh and me hooking up with our respective love interests stayed anchored deep in fantasy. But Leigh had a plan: Writing out what life could be like with our imaginary boyfriends in journals could make it come true. It was perfect timing, too, because my dad had just given me a tall book with "Ledger" stamped on the front and lime green lines on every page. Leigh named her journal after a fictitious British friend named "Emma." Leigh insisted the Benton lineage was part British. So she became obsessed with all things UK, from sipping Devonshire cream tea to spritzing lilac-scented toilet water imported from London on her sheets at night. For my journal, Leigh picked out the British-inspired name, Abbey. It was a lot easier to write in a journal when you felt like you were telling a friend your innermost secrets, especially an imaginary friend who lived in another country.

Every day, I wrote to Abbey about Dave. First, I filled the pages with true accounts of the time he took me to Hometowne Deli and made fun of the Hopkins students he called "Brains." Or about the time he took me to Crosley Square Café for lunch and taught me to sit directly across from my date instead of sliding all the way across the booth, away from my imaginary date. Then, Leigh and I spread a stack of magazines and catalogs on her bedroom floor and made collages out of pictures, words, and cartoons. After flipping through *The New Yorker* and *Town & Country* magazines, I was hard pressed to find the right furniture for Dave and me. So I dragged out the Sears catalog, where I found everything I needed in one place – pictures of brass beds, silk sheets, and machine-washable negligees. Meanwhile, Leigh glued a full-spread Calvin Klein ad in her journal that featured a woman on top of a man on a bed, while a mysterious wind blew their clothes off and forced one of her breasts to brave the storm like a zeppelin. Then, she peppered headlines like "Sexiest Weekend Fantasy" and "What He Really Wants" she clipped out of *Cosmopolitan* around the ad.

When summer hit, Leigh and I turned to smoking menthol cigarettes she stole from her dad's study, under the pretense that they kept the mosquitoes away. Every day, we stomped a path through the woods behind where new houses were being built on Bridlepath to a smooth rock that fit both of us like a loveseat. Just as I tasted the minty paper on my lips, two blonde peach fuzz heads popped up through the brush.

"It's my stupid brothers spying on us," I reported to Leigh. They ducked behind a tree and cackled with laughter.

"They need to work on their disguises," she said, blotting her lit cigarette out on the rock.

"They saw us, now my mother is going to kill me," I said flatly, bored with my mother's daily punishments. "Oh well." I lit up and took a drag anyway, watching my brothers dart out of the woods. I figured they were on their way to report my crime, but I was no longer afraid of what my mother would do to me. Being friends with Leigh filled me with a sense of independence and security. My mother could physically hurt me all she wanted, but that didn't change the fact that she was nothing to me but an enemy. Being around people who liked me sharpened my resolve that I could defy my fears that I was destined for complete failure and become someone one day.

"Your mother is such a bitch," Leigh said. We both laughed, then packed up.

"Guess I should prepare to die," I said.

"Parents might bruise you, but they can't really hurt who you are," Leigh said, swinging her backpack over her shoulder. Although it didn't make much sense to me at the time, it helped me walk into the fire with confidence.

When I got home, my brothers sat red-faced and bawling at the kitchen table. I figured I was next, so I just stood there, waiting for my punishment.

"Get the hell up to your room," my mother snapped. "This is none of your God damned business."

Yeah, okay. I walked backwards up to my room, afraid she'd hurl something at me, and locked the door like I did every day when I got home. Even with my door shut, I could hear everything she said. You could probably hear her yelling in the next county without any help from Nutone. I wondered if the police would show up this time.

"Which one of you little assholes stole my cigarettes?" she howled. "You think you wanna smoke? Well, now you're gonna smoke. Then you're going to eat this whole pack of cigarettes." Her voice sounded like a cross between a hurricane and our dog Nanda yelping, like the time she snagged her toenail on the track of the sliding glass door. Bruce gulped "No" in between crying and coughing.

"Keep smoking, you little bastard. Right now," she growled. Bruce started wailing. That'll teach them to quit following Leigh and me around. Then I realized what must have happened. They must have gotten the idea to try smoking from us, but got caught stealing her cigarettes. The amazing thing was they hadn't thought to tell on me. Bruce ratted on me daily, which fueled my intense desire to pummel him. The problem was he was the size of a refrigerator, and I was more like an ice cube tray. Matt kept to himself and rarely tattled. But both of them had a nasty habit of ticking off bullies, then promising, "My sister said she's going to beat you up," before hiding in the bushes. Thanks to them, I suffered my share of random snowball peltings. It must not have been my turn that day because she was focused only on them. When their torture was over, one bedroom door slammed, then another.

"You just wait 'til your father comes home," she hollered up the stairs.

I can't wait for Dad to come home, Bitch. I clamped my headphones over my ears and cranked up David Bowie to drown out the sound of my mother recounting the incident to my grandmother over the phone. That night, I found out Leigh walked into her own fire.

"Meet me at the trail," she choked between sobs. I ran down the trail thinking her parents found out about the back and front rubs and actually punished her. But when I got through the brush, I saw her mother through the kitchen window holding knives up high over the sink, then dropping them down in a crash of metal over and over again. We snuck in through the sliding glass doors and up to Leigh's room. Mrs. Benton drove her Gucci heels into the hardwood floors on the way to the living room where Mr. Benton slumped down in the leather chair and punched the TV power, bringing the crowd noise at the Orioles game to an abrupt end. "No baseball while I'm suffering," she wailed. Mr. Benton clicked the TV back on with the remote. "I said no baseball while I'm suffering, God damn you," Mrs. Benton's voice cracked in half and became a cry. Leigh winced. The crowd cheered, then went silent again.

Tears streamed down Leigh's face. Real ones, not acting tears. Once I saw her crying and tried to comfort her. But she shooed me away, explaining that she had dabbed Sea Breeze under her eyes to practice crying for a movie she was cast in. But this time was different. I wasn't sure what to make of the movie star turned little girl. It made me nervous, like seeing your father cry. We slumped down on the floor and I held her as her shoulders shook, two scared little girls, acting our age for once. "She's been drinking again," Leigh said. The sound of broken glass made Leigh cringe.

"Come on, let's go to my house," I said, vaguely aware that my house appeared to be safe by comparison. I'd never felt safe or secure in my house before. She nodded her head and we snuck back outside. Leigh spent the night, woke up, and went back through the trail to get ready for school without saying a word.

The next time I saw her, it was as if nothing had happened. But I could tell something had changed with the Bentons. Leigh rushed around, saying she had become just too consumed acting in a school play to come over after school anymore. Meanwhile, her mother had started working at a museum and seemed happier, walking around the house with a museum identification tag fluttering off a long necklace. I wondered if acting was like the pancake makeup Leigh smoothed on for the school play – thick enough to distort her age and convincing enough to hide the truth from everyone, including herself.

What Leigh said to me that day in the woods played over and over in my head: Parents might bruise you, but they can't really hurt who you are.

"My happy place relocated."

8 . SOLO FLYER

Summer was so loud. When the wind picked up, a sea of deep-green leaves churned the tree crowns, then rose all the way up to a symphony of furious swaying. Then, the trees swung like ancient pendulums, until they slowed to a stop. The leaves obscured everything, creating mini forests around each house. The temperature dropped as you drove up the steep hill by Broadmere Preparatory School. All because of the trees. For me, the trees signaled two things –time for Leigh to go shoot her series in California and time for me to leave Maryland for the land of no trees and all bugs, Florida. I wasn't thrilled about leaving Dave playing guitar all by himself with an audience of foliage, but hoped the Florida sun would bake me into a girl with a savage tan and boobs big enough to stop him in his tracks.

Every summer, my parents put me, not my brothers, on a plane to Grandmom and Papa Wasser's house. And every summer, my brothers whined, "Why can't we go? We wanna go to Disney World." "Because you'll bust up the place, that's why," my mother snorted through the cigarette pinched in one side of her mouth. Sure it wasn't fair to them, but I had to agree with my mother about my brothers' ability to detonate every room they entered and couldn't imagine my grandparents wrangling them. My mother's sisters branded me "spoiled" and lavished gifts on my brothers to make up for it. Bruce and Matt paraded the gifts around, chanting, "Only we got presents, not you." But when the stewardess slapped a "Solo Flyer" sticker on me that looked like a first place ribbon at the Maryland State Fair, I felt special and forgot all about their stupid presents.

I asked my grandmother why only I got sent to Florida, expecting to hear the "we can't handle your brothers" answer. But instead, she told me she was afraid my mother would literally kill me, just like the time she nearly strangled one of her sisters to death on the kitchen floor. I just stood there like a daddy long legs with its legs ripped off. My whole world shifted away and back. After that, she told me that my mother was sent to Dr. Schultz, a psychiatrist, until he suggested family therapy. "So I told him he's the one with the problem, not us, and took her right out of there," she said, taking a gulp of scotch. "Here, have an Eskimo Pie, sweetheart." My body felt like it was poured into place and was starting to set as she handed me the silver cube of ice cream.

It never really occurred to me to be afraid of my mother, except for that time she threatened to leave me on the side of I-95 driving home from Florida. I really thought she'd do it and had planned to hike to South of the Border and call my father. Instead of fearing her, I concentrated on defying her in every way possible. But the thought that she hated me enough to actually kill me made me sick and desperately sad at the same time. Was I really that bad of a kid? Was that what Bad Jackie meant? Biting the corner off the Eskimo Pie, my mind shifted back to reality and wondering what time *The Gong Show* came on.

Staying with my grandparents was like being an only child like Leigh, and it was heaven. If my grandparents found out I liked something, like Lender's Bagels, they'd stock up every flavor. An opened bag of Chips Ahoy would still be there two days later. Where I left it. That never happened at home. If you wanted food, you'd better eat out of the grocery bags in the car on the way home. I could leave my suitcase on the floor, and no one would raid it. Plus, my grandparents took me everywhere with them – from Disney World to seaside restaurants with their other retired friends. They never yelled at me once. The fact that they seemed delighted to have me around, just like my dad, made me feel better about myself, like maybe I was an okay kid and not the loser my mother said I was.

On Saturdays, Grandmom took me to work with her at the Sea Breeze Hotel. While she worked, the staff took me around, making me feel like Captain Stubing's daughter on *The Love Boat*. The maintenance man opened vending machines and handed me a Dr Pepper as he collected the money. The chef made me anything I wanted. Once he packed so many blueberries in my pancakes, they looked like hockey pucks. The tourist kids eyeballed me suspiciously when I carried my plate through the swinging doors right into the kitchen. The bartender let me refill my glass with the spray nozzle that squirted Cokes and pick cherries right out of the plastic container. After work, Grandmom took me out to lunch, then anywhere I wanted to go. Sometimes, we went to an arcade or shopping downtown. Everyone was so nice to me everywhere we went, it made me feel special and dread going home where I was anything but special. I wondered if Leigh always felt special because she got treated like that all the time.

Without using every finger, I could count the people who really loved me on one hand. Grandmom, Papa, and Dad. My grandmother liked to take credit for raising me when I was little, causing an emotional explosion from my mother. But it was true. When my mother went back to work, my grandmother watched me every day. She took me out to lunch, on bus rides, and on her weekly trip to the liquor store. Whenever I got sick, I could hear her calling into her job as a church bookkeeper to stay with me. Even now, I remember the relief washing over me, realizing she was staying home just to take care of me. If I spilled something, she said, "It's okay, honey," instead of slapping me. She practically cooed to me, "You are such a beautiful person, and don't you forget it." And when people asked her about me, she bragged that I was the most well-behaved child and that she was proud to take me anywhere. But my mother usually finished the sentence with, "Who are you kidding? She's a pain in the ass."

I remember Papa in his green work shirt bouncing me up and down on his knee, letting me eat M&M's and pickles at the kitchen table before dinner. He barely said a word, just like my dad, but led me around by the hand and showed me his medals from World War II. He called me Daisy and sang me a daisy song in German. When the Baltimore winters got too harsh for Papa's circulation, his doctor ordered him to move to a warmer climate. He filled his days tending to the lawn and reading *Reader's Digest*. Since they moved, Papa installed an in-ground sprinkler system, all by himself, an accomplishment he proudly pointed out to visitors.

My grandparents' ranch house perched high on a corner lot with orange and grapefruit trees dotted around what was left of the orchard that used to grow there. I thought it was so weird you could pull a grapefruit off a tree and eat it right there without stepping one foot in Winn Dixie. A circular driveway curved up in front of their Spanish red front porch where the lizards scampered all around a miniature tropical island sprouted up through the grass. Their living room was filled with cherub babies dipped in gold and a hanging lamp with oil dripping down and around another cherub baby who looked over his shoulder like he was ready to catch a football. Glass perfume bottles from Avon sculpted in the shapes of doves, frogs, and ladybugs filled with food coloring sat on the windowsills and reflected speckles of color on the stucco walls.

Down the hall in the back bedroom, I slept on the sleeper sofa near the rooster, a decanter that concealed my grandmother's scotch. When she thought no one was looking, she slipped back there, ducked under the cabinet with the Holy Bible displayed on top, unscrewed the rooster's head, and doused her ice with scotch. My grandparents didn't sleep in the same room. Instead Grandmom slept in the other back bedroom, while Papa slept in his recliner chair or out in the garage where he set up a sink and toilet for himself with only a piece of cardboard duct-taped to the floor as a makeshift wall for privacy. Except for watching television, they rarely occupied the same room. She called him "Dad" and talked about how she couldn't stand him when they first met. She worked as a bookkeeper for a trucking company; he drove the trucks. Then, after he left for the war and stopped calling her everyday, she said she fell madly in love with him.

After Grandmom left for work as a bookkeeper at the Sea Breeze Hotel and Motor Lodge, Papa and I fended for ourselves. I was just fine watching *The Price Is Right, The Love Boat,* and *The Gong Show* in that order, but Papa insisted I go everywhere with him, starting with shopping at Winn Dixie, The Beef People. The checkout stands spun like a record player, instead of the straight conveyor-belts in Maryland. No matter what we needed, he always bought the biggest tower of toilet paper in the free world. I looked for somewhere to hide as the skyscraper of toilet paper came around on the carousel and stopped. At that age, I feared we were messier than other families and required extensive amounts of toilet paper. But he probably just liked to buy mass quantities on sale.

After he presented his check, the lady stamped the back of the check and asked, "Place of employment, sir?" He stepped back. "Place of employment?"

he yelled. "I fought for my country. It's none of your damned business." After owning his own plumbing and heating company and rising up from poverty, he was outraged if anyone questioned his ability to pay for something. His military hair jetted straight up and the zinc oxide he smeared on his lips to deflect the scorching sun made a square outline around his mouth. Meanwhile, the clerk tilted the Tower de Papier, and it toppled into the cart like a building falling off a cliff.

Some days, he took me to the beach with him where the water was more lukewarm like the end of a bath than cool and refreshing. There were no waves in the Gulf of Mexico, just little splats on the sand like dropping a Dixie cup full of hot water on asphalt. I dug my toes into the soupy sand and carved clams out, earning me the nickname: Clam Digger. Then, we'd dump them in a bucket of water and lure their goopy bodies out of their shells by floating oatmeal on the surface. When trips to the hardware store got boring, Papa took me to visit his friends, where the inevitable fight broke out over which city had more history – Baltimore or Philadelphia. The Liberty Bell was always thrown out as the ultimate American Revolution symbol, with Papa saying, "Yeah, but you people don't know how to take care of history. That bell's got a crack in it." His friends leaned back in their metal lawn chairs, Sansabelt polyester slacks pulled over their huge bellies and up to their chins, red-faced, saying, "Aw, git outta here."

Eventually, he must have worried about finding new ways to entertain me, because he decided to enroll me at a day camp. I was afraid of going alone and begged Grandmom to let me just stay with Papa, vowing I would never ask to change the station from *The World at War* to *The Gong Show* again. But she said, "Oh, honey. Papa just doesn't know what to do with a little girl." She stared off into space as she towel-dried a frying pan. "You know, he always wanted a boy and had nothing to do with your mother." Then, she started getting mad. "Three daughters, and he brags he never changed a diaper, no sir." Meanwhile, another daddy long legs moment arrived, except with some kid searing my head with a magnifying glass when I realized I had been told the same story – that my mother was so furious I was a girl, she threw her IV bottle across the room. "That's why your mother got that ridiculous job as a cop. Trying to be like a boy so he'd love her. But instead, he's mad as hell at her for not staying home with you kids." The bucket load of information washed over me, but only a few items stuck. Papa's mad. Never changed a diaper. Doesn't like girls. Does that mean he doesn't like me, I wondered, devastated at the possibility. But for the rest of the summer, he acted the same as always, taking me swimming and horseback riding, proudly introducing me to his buddies, and running over the reflectors on the road to make me laugh.

The day I went to Waterfront Community Center, I missed my dad the most. He always made us the best lunches: sandwich with lunch meat that fit neatly into a fold-in Glad sandwich bag, UTZ potato chips, and one Tastykake quality cupcake product. Grandmom packed me a sandwich so heavy, it required a Winn Dixie full-sized grocery bag for transport to Waterfront. So much meat was stuffed into the bread, it bulged in the middle like a speed bump. The sandwich was so wide, she used a Ziploc freezer storage bag instead of the smaller one Dad would use. Plus, she wrapped a Coke in aluminum foil like I was going on a field trip.

When I unrolled the bag, a crowd of wide-eyed kids circled around me. Usually, when kids gathered around, it was to see my dad's daily message. But this time was different, and my jaw clenched as more kids climbed onto the picnic table to watch. When I opened the sandwich, clumps of meat plopped on the table, and the kids snatched them up like seagulls. The crowd of kids grew as other kids left their tables to see what I had. I dropped the sandwich and Coke in the trash can and ran as fast as I could to the beach. Behind me, the trash can flipped over as they fought over the sandwich.

As I walked down the beach back to the community center, I fought back tears and tried to figure out a way I could hide all day behind the community center until Papa came back to get me. Those kids didn't have any food at all, I realized, feeling incredibly lucky. In Baltimore, I was on the bottom rung of the ladder. Here, I was the rich one. It wasn't lost on me how completely different I was from those kids and how incredibly privileged, just because I had something to eat. At the same time, I wondered if Leigh felt sorry for me the way I felt sorry for them, that I wasn't as high class or as smart as her. As sure as the thump of seagull poop that nailed me in the head just then, I realized Leigh would never see me as an equal, no matter what.

As soon as I discovered the gymnastics mats at Waterfront, everything got better. All day long, I tumbled until I got bored because there was no other gymnastics equipment to practice on. Then, I noticed teenage girls learning a dance on stage. Performing on stage like that seemed unattainable, something only people meant for success like Leigh could do. Every day, I followed along from the floor and learned every move when suddenly, the instructor kicked a girl out for fooling around. In slow motion, she turned to me and asked me to take her place. Just like that, I was on stage doing the "Fire Dance" with teenage girls. It was my big chance to become a star like Leigh.

Overjoyed, Grandmom took me to the mall to buy a red leotard and the dance record, *Fire* by The Ohio Players. But when she spotted the nude woman wrapped in a see-through fire hose on the cover, she leaned backward. "Oh, I don't know about this," she said, as if I would suddenly get the idea to strip down, wrap the garden hose around me, and do my fire dance in the front yard, shocking the retirees. "Well, okay then," she said and bought it anyway so I could practice at home.

At the Waterfront Community Center Talent Show, I wrapped aluminum foil around my wrists and ankles and performed the Fire Dance, then changed into my aqua Danskin leotard with the glow-in-the-dark stripes and threw a round-off and eight back handsprings in a straight line. When I bounced up to Grandmom and Papa at the end of the show, Papa greeted me with: "You're going to kill yourself." His zinc oxide made a faint thin line around his lips. Grandmom leaned back, clasped her hands and said, "You were wonderful. I really thought you were on fire." It felt alien hearing praise instead of how bad I looked, or that I embarrassed them in some way. Then, she knelt down and looked me in the eye. "My mother told me I was only fit to scrub floors, but not you. You are special," she grabbed my shoulders. "You are going to make something of yourself one day."

Since the fire dance, I made all new friends at Waterfront. But every day, I thought about how much I missed Dave, until I met Timothy, the cutest, most popular guy at Waterfront. With his dark, curly hair and deep blue eyes like a mood ring, he was like a kid version of Paul Michael Glaser, and I wanted to "go with him" so bad. I sat in one of the chairs that lined the walls waiting for my turn at pool, and ice ran through my veins when Timothy suddenly ran his hand along my leg.

"Feel this. It's so smooth, it's disgusting," he told his chubby friend whose face looked like bumpy chicken skin. My excitement collapsed as his friend rubbed my leg, too.

"Yeah, really," they both laughed.

After I played pool, I walked through the breezeway toward the gym when Timothy popped his head around the corner. "Hey, Jackie, come here."

The sun threw a sheet of light at me so bright, I had to walk over to the side of the building and wait for my eyes to focus. When I rounded the corner, I saw that Timothy wasn't alone. His jerky friend was standing there with his arms dangling nervously to the side like a cartoon octopus with a crooked smile on his face. My instinct told me to run, but my body froze. In one quick move, Timothy pinned me against a tree and caught my hair up on the bark, but my screams lodged in my throat like a cough drop. He tilted his head to one side and covered his mouth over mine. My body wilted and tingled as he slid one warm hand up my shirt and pressed me further into the palm tree. My body went numb, and his friend shoved both hands all the way up my shirt and pinched the nubs on my chest hard. I knew I should have screamed because it hurt, but I couldn't feel anything but confusion as my body slipped out of itself, leaving a shell behind.

"Hey, what are you kids doing over there?" Judy, the white-haired, pink-lipsticked lady who ran Waterfront yelled. The way she dressed in her double-knit polyester suit with vinyl sandals and hose, I almost thought she was my grandmother. "You boys get out of here," she said. "You come with me," she said as she dug her hot pink fingernails into my Busch Gardens "Ride the Python" t-shirt and dragged me to her office.

She swung the metal door open to her office that looked like the inside of a refrigerator, all white and cold. An orange plastic vase sat on her desk with dusty, artificial roses sticking out of it at awkward angles. The door opened again, and Otis, the janitor, came in to "have a talk with me." His gray beard danced like a show cat as he used words like "Promiscuous" and "Reputation." Questions tumbled around in my head. Is it okay that I liked it that Timothy picked me to kiss, since he was most popular and a total fox? Why was his stupid friend there? Why am I in trouble and not them? My conclusion: I really am Bad Jackie.

Luckily, no one ever told my grandparents, Timothy still came to Waterfront, but avoided me for the rest of the summer, and his chicken-skin friend stopped coming to Waterfront. Instead of realizing that getting pinned against a tree by two boys was a dangerous situation, I romanticized it – a pathetic pattern I would repeat for years to come. Over and over, I played Timothy kissing me, except I imagined that I was the model in the Calvin Klein ad Leigh put in her journal. Timothy was the man leaning into me. Just like the ad, my boob was showing, except I made myself laugh because I didn't have one. Timothy's warm hand is on my belly, moving up. I took care to record every second of my encounter in my journal, leaving out Timothy's stupid friend.

The minute the airplane door opened in Baltimore, I bolted up the jetway holding my new Ohio Players album and jumped into my dad's arms. His jaw dropped when he saw the album, and he said he couldn't believe "You're almost a teenager now." He hugged me and held my hand all the way to Baggage Claim while I whirled around and showed him my Fire Dance moves. When we got home, I handed each of my brothers a Donald Duck hat with a bill that quacked. They furiously squeaked the hats until they split the plastic bills open, letting out one last pssst. When I distributed the rest of the Disney toys and set the bag on the floor, my mother screamed at me for putting the bag on the floor. Any excitement I had about seeing my dad evaporated, and I headed straight up to my room.

"What the hell's wrong with her?" she said. I sat on the stairs and eavesdropped.

"Huh?" Dad said, having no idea I left upset.

"What the hell does she have to be upset about? I'll tell you one thing, if she doesn't get an attitude adjustment, I'm sending her straight to see that psychiatrist, Dr. Schultz."

I gulped air in, realizing that was the same psychiatrist my grandmother sent my mother to after she supposedly tried to kill her sister. Then, I screamed, "Go ahead, send me to Dr. Schultz. I don't care." Because I hate coming home to you. She obviously didn't make the connection between her badgering me and my emotional state.

She laughed out loud, saying, "Did you hear that, Gary?" But it sounded like: "Chew hear that Gary?" Dad said nothing, and no one took me to Dr. Schultz.

At the time, I was too young to realize my life was playing out as if it had been scripted. Generation after generation, the script and ending had stayed the same. Only the players changed. It was all up to me to change the plot and make my own ending.

> *"Well, that's enough about my life.*
> *Guess I'll tell a joke now."*

9 . THE TRUTH LIST HURTS

The Rear Admirer gay club posted a sign that read: "Enter through the rear, Captain" on the front of the building, so it was no wonder none of the straight male comics dared to audition at open mic there. For me, performing at a gay men's bar was refreshing, welcome territory. Compared to the male-dominated southern audiences I encountered, gay audiences were whip-smart, appreciative of the writing, and not at all afraid to pound the tables with laughter. Plus they flat out went wild over my Barbie jokes. After signing up thirty-five times at the male-dominated Yuk before earning my first five-minute chance on stage, I grew frustrated encountering the same chauvinism I dealt with working at muffler world. Not once did I feel discriminated against for being a straight girl wearing not enough make-up at the Admirer. Instead, people at the Rear Admirer treated me with respect.

Each week, the Admirer featured a contest and allowed comics five-minute sets. Then, the audience voted. If you won, you'd open for the Sally Ho Drag Show over the weekend. My first night out, a gay male comic endeared himself to the audience immediately. With hair swooped up like soft-serve ice cream and enormous blue eyes, he announced that he was the grown-up version of Herbie the Elf from the vintage Frosty the Snowman film, and the place went nuts. He beat me hands down with that one. But after a few weeks auditioning there, my jokes about Barbie and Bionic Woman killed, and I won first shot opening for the Sally Ho Drag Show.

As I watched a dressing room bustle with drag queens getting ready for the show, I panicked about how bland I looked. With thick fake lashes, rhinestone-studded eye make-up, and dramatic feather plumes, the drag queens paraded around like glamorous Vegas show girls. I looked more like an intern at the public library. So I thought I'd start my set by calling attention to my dullness right away.

"You guys look more like women than I do," I said, drawing absolute silence and blinky doe eyes from the audience. I had yet to discover drag show etiquette – drag queens are to be identified as women when they're in drag. And, I had yet to realize the duality of the situation I was in – trying to shine on the outside while feeling dull on the inside. Realizing my terrible mistake, I shifted quickly into another joke: "My friends say I look like the Little Dutch Boy…I go to the paint store and kids are pointing, 'Hey, Mom! Look, get him to autograph our paint can.' Good start-your-set laughter. After the show, a man ran over to me, "Oh my God, you have to add this to your Dutch Boy joke. Say, 'But I've never had my finger in a dyke.'" Since I started stand-up, I purposefully stayed away from "blue comedy," anything vile, disgusting, or profane I normally said everyday. I tucked his suggestion in my back pocket in case I ever needed to save myself on stage with a dead ringer.

When I walked off stage, a cold beer waited for me from the bartender. After the show, the DJ, who called himself "Sister Tim," walked me to my car since it was in a marginally dangerous neighborhood. The Admirer was but one venue I frequented at the time. Stage time was stage time, if you asked me. I wasn't above following angry poet slam participants at rec centers, harmonica soloists at coffee houses, or toddler tantrums at picnics. Performing up to five nights a week empowered me to develop more material and earn precious experience. In less than one year, I had performed over 100 times all around Atlanta and the south and won second place in a radio station's comedy contest.

Without realizing it, I had transferred my addictive behavior to comedy, living off the high of performing up to five nights a week, then crashing back down in depression when I got home. It probably wasn't such a great idea to seek validation from people who considered exceeding the three-drink minimum an accomplishment. But making people laugh made me feel like everything wrong with me was okay, and I couldn't get enough. When I wasn't performing, I forced myself through the day, anxious to get back on stage and let the roar of the crowd validate my very existence. But when people approached me after shows, saying things like: "I had a really bad day, and you just made it so much better," I also felt like I was delivering a social service of sorts. Meanwhile, I remained oblivious to the danger of the traps I was setting for myself by cultivating material from my personal life.

Comics looked to all kinds of sources for material – the news, daytime television, and any physical deformities there was no way the audience could overlook. All sorts of tricks helped comics produce material. Some people relied on "Ranting," which meant tape recording yourself while spouting off about something, like traffic, then pulling jokes out of the tape. Ranting worked for me for a while, until I got on my own nerves. "The Truth List," which involved writing the most searing truths about your life and twisting the information into jokes, worked best for me. The more brutal the truth, the more powerful the jokes, I thought.

Addictive patterns, starting with alcohol, underscored my entire life. So I started with the truth statement: I was poured from two generations of alcoholics and wrote the joke: "The other night, my friends got so wasted playing quarters and I'm like, 'Look, Grandmom, if you're going to drink my friends under the table, at least bring your own beer.'"

Learning in therapy that my family was alcoholic wasn't so much of a surprise. My mother's mother, Grandmom Wasser, told dramatic stories of bootlegging in the back of a car as a little girl and holding a hammer ready to bust open a ceramic jug of moonshine she called "the good stuff." If the cops pulled them over, her job was to bash the jug open and let the "good stuff" drain out of the holes in the floorboard. By the end of her life, she had become so heavily immersed in alcohol, the truth for her swirled like liquid, evaporating at the corners and running off, leaving me with nothing solid to believe as I listened to her stories. Meanwhile, my father's parents, the Eberstarkers, drank cheap beer literally every day starting at lunch and claiming: "It's three o'clock somewhere." They once dragged a cooler filled with National Bohemian beer to my brother's little league game, then cheered for the wrong kid. Behind them, a sign read:

"Absolutely No Alcohol."

Growing up Catholic meant a guaranteed chug of wine at mass and portable mini-bar for church socials. My parents toted a small suitcase to parties that opened up to reveal a small bar with leather straps that held hard alcohol and all the proper bartending tools, yet I never saw my mother drunk. But when Dad drank, he'd end up running around the woods searching for his friend, Jack Daniels, and telling my mother off. He once got so drunk, he told my mother: "Shove a pudding pop up your ass, bitch," making my brothers and me howl for years to come.

As for me, growing up with such easy access to alcohol, so I already had plenty of drinking experience, but had come dangerously close to alcoholism when I dragged my college drinking habits to the real world of Atlanta. Driving home blinding drunk one night, I nearly headed down the wrong side of the highway. In my peripheral vision, I saw a line of state trooper cruisers along the highway, but they didn't notice me as I gripped the steering wheel, somehow kept the car straight, and avoided killing someone.

Realizing the gravity of what I had done the next morning was the jolt that kept me from driving drunk again. Then, repeated warnings from a recovered alcoholic who also happened to be a psychic resonated with me: "You will severely regret what you could have accomplished if you keep drinking this way." At the time, I could almost feel the pain of letting my life slip away. So I turned my drinking way down to the occasional range. Noticing comics around me who required alcohol before going on stage made me feel relieved for myself that I did not rely on anything but memory before going up there, but terrified for them.

After cutting back on alcohol, I transferred my alcohol addiction first to bad relationships, then to therapy. After "graduating" from so much therapy, I thought I was cured now that I knew for sure that I was a depressed, emotionally insecure young woman with post-traumatic stress issues, and alcoholic tendencies. The truth statement: I'm a therapy connoisseur helped me craft the joke: "I've been in therapy over five years to get over my fear of being trapped in a box...with a mime." A few years after I had moved to Atlanta, Grandmom Eberstarker died, my fiancé got another woman pregnant, and my father was about to get remarried and become a father to his wife's daughter. The way I saw it, Dad was the only person left who really loved me and he was about to get a new daughter who would surely replace me. Feeling completely alone and desperate, I took on therapy the way some people obsess over a new hobby. I didn't just seek healing, I attacked it, attending therapy sessions, devouring self-help books, and weeping at workshops.

When I tired of books that started with: "When Will I Change (Fill in blank)," or "Ten Steps to a More (Insert adjective) You," I headed for weekend-long retreats. I desperately wanted to take responsibility and create the life I wanted, but I didn't know how. So I asked my therapist for homework assignments after every session that ranged from writing journals to writing letters to people like my mother for railing me and my father for standing idly by as she beat my spirit down, then setting the paper on fire. Seeing flames lick the words, then curl them in on themselves felt deliciously therapeutic, until the smoke alarm went off.

My most intense homework assignment was to research the past to understand the origin of my family and gain insight on why they made certain decisions, like why did my mother hate me? Why did a woman who hated children have three? How did my parents end up together in the first place?

Sitting at a tiny café table in my apartment on day, my dad explained the "how" of everything…How he met my mother at a wedding after breaking up with his girlfriend Paula. How he thought she was a funny, smart, nice person to spend the rest of his life with. How he didn't listen when my mother's twin sisters pleaded with him not to marry her because she was anything but funny, smart, or nice. How when they got home from the honeymoon, my mother stopped showering. Stopped caring. How my father put a gun to his head and threatened to kill himself if she didn't get it together. How she suddenly got pregnant with me. How she told his parents she would take everything, including the baby, if my father ever left her. How, after I was born September, 1966, my father was over his head in financial trouble. And how, in God's name, my parents managed to have two more children.

"So how come you didn't point the gun at her?" I asked. He laughed out loud and said it never occurred to him.

"She told me I was a mistake," I told him, still cringing from even saying the words.

"Best mistake I ever made," he said, putting his hand on my cheek and making the pain evaporate. The other two weren't exactly planned either, he said. Being the kind of man visibly delighted by children, he might have been daunted by the financial responsibility, but still overjoyed.

When the subject turned to me, he said he didn't know I was unhappy, that I called my mother "Mommy," and seemed "happy as a lark." That's when it hit me. We both struggled with postcard traumatic stress disorder, the habit of capturing only happy memories in our minds like a vacation postcard and leaving all the reality out of the picture. Pink sunsets frozen on a postcard don't happen every day. And, even my dad liked to joke: "Not every day can be Disney World, you little creeps." Either he had no idea his wife was thrashing us kids around while he was at work, or maybe he only remembered how we looked happy when he came home.

Maybe that explained why I made so many bad choices in relationships. Then, I'd capture the "good times" on a postcard and carry that around, conveniently forgetting how it felt to be locked out of his trailer in the rain or have my ass grabbed in front of my grandmother. When something bad happened, I clutched the postcard to my chest and convinced myself things would be good again. But carrying the comedy postcard around all day, to convince myself comedy was the only thing I needed wore thin. Soon my friends wrote a Truth Statement of their own: "You are using comedy to avoid dating." When my friends noticed I had been ignoring advances by the opposite sex, they urged me to give a particular male admirer a chance because "he's a nice guy." My instincts told me differently.

The first time I met Aston, his geeky machine-gun laughter and the way he cornered me freaked me out. So I fled out the back of the bar, ran to my car, and forgot all about him, on purpose. When my friend Meredith later invited me to go with her to see a movie at his apartment, I reluctantly went.

The minute Aston opened the door to greet us, I started doubting my initial impression of him. Gone was the cackling laughter. Instead, he appeared self-assured and professional. When Aston shook my hand, it felt warm and equal.

Men at Muffler International would never issue an equal handshake to a woman, so I appreciated it. Glancing around his apartment, I noticed beautiful honey wood floors and modern era chrome furniture. His stock started going up for taste, until I noticed the pungent odor of cat urine punching through French vanilla-scented Glade. Realizing he was a cat person sent the stock plunging back down. But when he and his friends attended to our every whim like true gentlemen, I started doubting my initial instinct about him. During the movie, I found myself checking out his wavy chocolate hair and studying his angular shoulders. He looked exactly like a man leaning off a sailboat in a Hopper painting. At the end of the night, he asked me out and I heard myself say yes as a pang of nausea hit my stomach. I'd realize the power of listening to your instincts soon enough. For now, I doubted myself.

At first, we seemed to have a lot in common, except money. His father had invented something earth-changing; his mother, a wildly successful painter. He had instant access to a seemingly bottomless bank account while I struggled to support myself and felt proud that I had not asked my dad for money since he helped me set up utilities when I first moved to Atlanta. His mother told him he was a mistake. Ditto. He grew up in an affluent part of Maryland. Me too.

"You're intoxicating, you know that?" he said, leaning over to kiss me one summer night on my front porch with lightning bugs blinking between the trees like tiny caution lights.

"I don't think we should do this tonight," I said, as he gently fumbled at my bra.

"I think we should, too," he said, leading me into the bedroom as I felt myself fly out of my body, leaving only a shell behind again. After my last relationship, I swore I would not yield my whole being to a boyfriend in hopes of him taking away my problems and allowing me to drop mine, then live his life. According to one of my many self-help books, once a woman tosses the idea that happiness comes from someone else, she can experience true love. The first time we slept together, I was blind to the fact that I had already yielded to him and left my instinct and myself behind. Instead, I felt giddily happy and convinced myself I was in love with him.

We acted as if we were tragically in love, both treading the same path trying to shed the past and change our lives. When we went on dates, I went along with what Aston wanted to do: camped, dined at expensive restaurants, and watched guy movies he wanted to see. Whenever I did stand-up, he never watched the show, but took me to a French bakery for dessert afterward. We were like two bruised pears huddled together comparing our pasts except when the bruises touched, the damage spread. We were just too busy being "in love" to notice.

"So I got a Miracle Bra...
Apparently, it's going to take more than that."

10 . THE LAST DOUBLEMINT TWIN

The Florida sun baked everything but my boobs, so I stuffed some tissue into my training bra to plump them up, put on my new gauze purple halter dress and straw hat studded with sea shells, and headed out to the driveway to see if Dave was playing his guitar. I imagined him looking up just long enough to see my hat poke through the brush, revealing a young Stevie Nicks, then freeze in love. But when I came through the woods, only the Graysons' mutt, Cookie, was sprawled out in the driveway, farting in her sleep. No Dave. So I ripped my hat off, tore the tissue out of my bra, and ran down to Leigh's house.

As I peeked in the glass door to see if Leigh was home, she yelled, "Oh my God, Bad Jackie is back. Get in here." She seemed genuinely excited to see me and gave me a hug. Just then, a girl wearing an indigo Indian shirt, three necklaces, three earrings in each ear, and leather strap sandals drifted into the room.

"This is Nickie from California." You could tell she wasn't from Millwood, with her blonde curly hair all wiry and wild instead of curled under like a mushroom. The excited girl energy reached a feverish pitch as we caught up on our respective summers. Then, Mrs. Benton popped her head in, saying she had to go to the store and did we want to go to Friendly's Ice Cream for a while? Leigh and I popped up, but Nickie just said, "What's a 'Friendly'?"

All three of us ordered fishbowls full of ice cream with chunks of Snickers so heavy, they slid down the chocolate syrup like drunk skiers. The minute I started using "schmick," a word Leigh and I invented before I left, Nickie cracked up and uncontrollably, snorting streams of ice cream all over the table. A cross between schmuck and dick, "schmick" worked nicely to skate close to saying a cussword without getting in trouble. When I called her "Schmicky Nickie," she doubled over, mopping the tabletop with her spirally hair. Leigh got quiet, sat her spoon on the table, and leaned back in the booth, seething. But Nickie and I kept going. Eventually, Leigh stood up, walked to the phone booth in the back, and called her mother to pick us up earlier than planned.

Nickie and I were too busy laughing to fully realize how incensed Leigh had become. Leigh and Nickie had planned to go to Crosley Square after dinner. But when Nickie asked if I could go, too, Leigh shot her a look and said she suddenly didn't feel like going. Just like that, I was propelled from the group like a module off a rocket. When Nickie sent me magazine ads of models with spiders drawn on their faces and funny captions of how "schmicky" they were and how they must eat at the "schmicketeria," I was surprised. I figured Leigh would have told Nickie I was a loser or something. I showed Leigh the letter, but she just twisted her hair and said, "It's not even that funny." Just like that, Leigh stopped returning my calls and inviting me over, but she wouldn't tell me why, and I was afraid to ask.

Months went by, no Leigh. Then, out of nowhere, she invited me to go to a party in Haven Park with her. She said her mother was making her go, which meant the party would be a total bore. But I was so thrilled she asked me to go, I jumped like a kangaroo through the trail to her house.

Leigh had just been shopping and had spread all of her new clothes across the bed in her parents' room. Only once had I been in that room to return a sleep machine Leigh took from Mr. Benton's bedside table so we could listen to the ocean sounds it produced. That was the only time I ever heard Mr. Benton say something. He actually yelled, "Leigh, you don't just waltz in here and take whatever you damn well please." But that was exactly what she did.

I flipped through the clothes on the bed as she leaned her head in her hand, bored and paging haphazardly through *The New Yorker*. Without looking up, she said I could wear anything I wanted, so I picked out a purple velour top with satin grapes on the front. She picked the emerald green version of the same shirt I picked out. "We're twins," I said buzzing with excitement. "Right," she said, swatting my words flat like a fly.

Mrs. Benton drove us to Haven Park in their station wagon with the

"Breighton School" sticker on the back. I wondered if people thought I was a private school girl just because I was riding in the car. When Mrs. Benton drove, she floored the gas, then drifted. Floored. Drifted. Floored. Drifted. By the time we got there, I felt seasick.

We pulled up in front of a Spanish-style house on top of a hill. A maze of brick walkways and gardens stacked up in front of the house like tiers of a wedding cake. We both froze when we realized the party stopped, and everyone was looking at us from one of the patios. Just then, I remembered, Oh yeah, they're staring because the movie star has arrived.

"Let's just go," Leigh said just as someone on the patio mocked, "Oh look, it's the Doublemint twins." I felt as embarrassed as if everyone in the party found out I was wearing Sears underwear. Leigh's irritation seared into me, sucking the excitement out of me and making me want to burst into tears right there. Sometimes, I felt like she just hated me.

"We should never be twins again," Leigh scolded me, clenching the words between her teeth as if wearing the shirts were my idea. I followed behind her as she climbed the steps. Leigh said she didn't know the kid who was having the party. The minute I heard his mother roll her tongue and pronounce "Sprite" as if it were French, I classified the party as "phony."

"What a bunch of dweebs," Leigh said. "Call Dave and get us a ride home." Dutifully, I used the phone in the kitchen to call the Graysons. My heart plunged when Peter answered. Dave wasn't home, but Peter said he'd be right there. Fifteen minutes later, he roared up in his Porsche with the top down and screeched to a cartoon stop. We took off running down the stairs, making the party freeze again, then jumped into his car laughing our heads off.

"Thank you, thank you. You saved us," Leigh announced, stretching her arms wide like an opera singer, then swooping down and kissing him right on the cheek. I couldn't believe she just kissed an adult like he was her boyfriend or something. Peter blushed and punched the gas, sucking us down into the leather seat and blasting the party from sight.

When we got to the Graysons, Peter carefully pulled his Porsche into the garage and invited us in. Mr. and Mrs. Grayson were out and only his friend from college, Frank, sat on the sofa watching TV with the two dogs at his feet. "Come 'ere, girls," Peter said, sounding a lot like Charlie on *Charlie's Angels*. He plopped me on one knee and Leigh on the other. "Look at me, I've got two babes." Frank laughed nervously like the chicken-skin boy at Waterfront, sending a quick wave of nausea through me. I could understand why Leigh got picked to sit on his knee, but not me. Then, I concluded that since Leigh was famous, he only included me because he didn't want to make me feel bad.

We stayed as long as we could at the Graysons because Leigh's mother thought we were still at the party. Someone must have called her as soon as we left, because when we got back to Leigh's, she was furious, growling, "Those were very influential people. How dare you embarrass me?"

"You can't expect me to like them, Mom," Leigh shot back. "This is not California, and they are not my friends. I can't believe you made me go to that stupid, geek party." Again, I stood there, amazed she could let her mother have it like that. I pulled the Doublemint shirt over my halter dress and handed it to Leigh. As I pushed my way back through the leaves in the trail, I heard Leigh and her mother arguing, followed by a single door slam. I imagined Leigh slammed it in her mother's face again and wished I had the nerve to do that.

Weeks went by before Leigh called me again. "Only when she wants something," Mrs. Grayson called over her shoulder as she dove her hands in the murky sink again. But since I didn't have any other friends to hang out with in the neighborhood, I jumped whenever she called me. One night, she asked me to help her get ready for a party. So I ran down there and helped her set out plastic liters of Coke on her dining room table and dumped bags of chips in deep wooden salad bowls. When we were done, she informed me I wasn't invited. On some level, I knew I should have been upset by that, but the thought was another stream of liquid across parched soil. Some liquid absorbed, some didn't. All that was left was dust-covered confusion. I blew it from my mind and headed straight to the Graysons to avoid letting any emotion at all surface.

"That's just terrible," Mrs. G said as she snapped on a bracelet that was actually a broken watch with a peacock feather fanned across the face. On Saturday nights, the Graysons always went out to dinner downtown. I wanted to cry because it was one of those nights I could either go home to my room and be miserable with nothing to do, or stay at the Graysons and watch TV with the dogs.

"You deserve better. You'll find a nice friend. Why don't you stay here and watch TV. The boys will be home soon," she said, giving my shoulders a quick squeeze. Besides Grandmom Wasser, Mrs. G showed me what having a mom could be like. She loved me as if I were her daughter. She always welcomed me and never made me feel stupid. And she listened, always. Even when she was having a conversation with another adult, she went out of her way to include me.

"Where are the boys?" I asked, careful not to just ask about Dave.

"Dave went out with some unlucky girl. Peter went to throw his money away at Pimlico."

"Oh."

"I feel so bad for you, honey. You listen to me, that Leigh is not a nice girl. Don't you forget that you are a nice girl," she said, patting me on the head as she said, "nice girl." Her words warmed me like hot tea. But the feeling quickly turned lukewarm as I figured I really must be Bad Jackie and Mrs. G was just saying that because she felt sorry for me. I heard people downstairs and my heart fluttered, hoping Dave was home. But it was Peter and his friend stammering around the kitchen, eating pretzels. Peter sounded so loud and friendly, I knew he had to be drunk.

"Hey, Jackie," he said as if he were announcing my name on *The Tonight Show*. "Come 'ere and sit on my lap." Stunned by his attention because Leigh, the real star, wasn't there, I reluctantly walked over to him. Frank's nervous laughter hammered at the air. Suddenly, I felt special as he pulled me onto his lap, like maybe Peter did like me better than Leigh. Was that possible? Maybe Peter was the only person in the United States who thought I was prettier than Leigh. Or maybe Peter lost his contact lenses.

"So, what do you and Davey do when you're alone, huh?" Peter asked with a "dare you to tell me" sideways look.

"What?" my head flew back, making me lose my balance and almost land on my back. Peter caught me with his arm and set me upright. It felt nice to be caught. Safe.

"He grabs ya, doesn't he? Come on, you can tell me," he said, shaking me like the answer would just fall out like a coin out of a vending machine.

"He doesn't do anything." My face felt like a boiled tomato about to split open.

"Sure he doesn't."

Mr. and Mrs. G crossed the living room, gathering keys and slipping on their coats. "You leave her alone," she said, clipping on an earring. "Leigh is having a party and didn't invite Jackie, and that's just horrible."

"That little bitch," Peter said, surprising me with his anger. He was standing up for me. Suddenly, I felt like I had a home. After the Graysons left in Mr. G's new Jaguar and Frank got up to go to the bathroom, Peter slipped his hand under my shirt and pressed his face into the back of my neck. His razor stubble scratched against my neck as his other hand squeezed my thigh through my blue silk shorts.

"You know I love you, don't ya? You're my baby." A flash of heat engulfed me as he kissed my hair. Meanwhile, confusion swelled my brain. *Why does he like me? How come Dave doesn't like me this way? But he's older than Dave, how can he possibly like me?* His tongue pressed against the back of my neck, making my skin go prickly. With one quick shove, Peter slid me off his lap onto the sofa as Frank walked around the corner. My body was soaked in sweat, and I worried they could tell. When they got up to go in the kitchen, I ran home, went straight up to my room, and changed my clothes. What just happened with Peter dropped out of my immediate awareness and into an abyss, as if it happened everyday. Leigh's party was all I could think about. So I shut the lights off and started spying.

Both sets of sliding glass doors to the living room and dining room opened and closed as kids ran in and out. The living room lit up like a lantern with kids buzzing around the disco ball. Leigh darted around on the deck between the glass doors in her Danskin leotard and matching wrap skirt swirling around - a moth trying to bust through a screen. A cluster of girls formed on the back deck. But when Leigh got near them, they dispersed and quickly went inside. I wondered if Leigh noticed she was the reason why.

As summer came to an end, the trees grew quieter as the leaves spiraled to the ground. Faded *Seventeen* magazines littered the pool patio as the air cooled, making way for fall. When I returned home after my last day of hanging out at the pool, something was terribly wrong. My mother was home, but the house was quiet. I crept into the kitchen, and there she was, sitting alone at the table, smoking. Besides screaming, cigarette smoke was her preferred mode of communication. Short bursts of smoke blown straight ahead in an invisible line meant something was funny. A quick puff that suspended a single cloud in the air meant disbelief. One line of smoke like a boiling teakettle meant she was furious and that a strike was eminent.

The minute she saw me, she spurted out one quick, violent plume, then smashed her cigarette down. "I have a bone to pick with you, Lady Jaquelyn." She really thought that name offended me; but since it sounded like royalty, I took it more as a compliment. "Stupid Bitch" was the one that stung. "Fat Ass" was the one that left a mark because it only confirmed what kids at the pool called me: "Bumble Butt."

"I found your little diary while I was cleaning," she said. My stomach dropped out like I was on a roller coaster. Then, I got a quick flash of what must have happened: She yanked my bed away from the wall to clean the window, and my diary popped open right on the carpet. I could just see her stopping her cleaning right there, unwrapping a fresh pack of Marlboros, tapping cigarette after cigarette out of the pack, and reading it cover to cover while sending out smoke signals - dotted humor lines punctuated by furious bursts as she devoured every word.

Her hand felt like a steel claw as she dug her nails into the back of my neck and shoved me up the stairs. My journal sat embarrassed on my bed, open and naked. I sucked in a puff of air, and she slammed me up against the Nutone speaker. The robin's-egg-blue-on-sky-blue flowered wallpaper she smoothed up on my walls despite my pre-teen protests about such little girlie décor blurred.

"I read about your little boyfriends and your little crush on Davey," she said with a smirk like she was a girl my age picking on me at recess. *Oh great, now she'll tell Dave all about the Sears collage of love* I made with pictures of brass beds, satin sheets, and polyester lingerie. My stomach plunged just thinking about Dave finding out about it. The hatred I felt for my mother sparked a fire that sent a single wisp of smoke spiraling through me. The pressure would only build from there. My life is none of your God damned business. My jaw muscles throbbed as I grit my teeth while she hissed threats into my ears: "You sneaky little slut. You let boys feel you up in Florida. I'm calling your grandparents right now to tell them what you did. You'll never go down there again. And I read what you wrote about me and you'd better watch it, Lady Jaquelyn. I'll ground you for the rest of your fucking life if you ever write one more word."

    She shoved me on the bed, slammed the door, and stomped down the stairs with her lower lip thrust out like a child's. My journals were filled with so many dreams, I honestly didn't remember writing about her, but I must have called her "Bitchface" or something. Heat encased my throat as I stifled tears. I refused to let her threats make me cry. From my room, I heard her calling my grandmother and talking extra special loud so I could hear every word about "what I do with boys." To add even more drama, she repeated my grandmother's reaction: "I know you're shocked. I know you can't believe your Jackie did that. I know you're disappointed in her. Don't worry, she's never coming to Florida again." My eyes burned as if they got lemon juice squeezed in them as I tried not to cry. But I wiped the few tears that escaped away and sunk into myself to make a plan. If I didn't get that journal out of there immediately, she'd steal it again and show it to Davey and Mrs. G to get a good laugh, except she would be the only one laughing. The horror of my mother finding my journal again eclipsed any fear of Leigh reading them. I figured she wouldn't waste her time. Looking back, I wished I would have buried it in the backyard. At least I could have found it again one day. It's astounding to me that Leigh could have so little regard for my feelings. Was I that wrong about her that she actually cared about me? Or did she really ever care about anyone?

    Just like when we first moved to Millwood, I stretched out flat on my bed and waited for Leigh's station wagon to stop, go, stop down her driveway. Even though Leigh and I weren't friends anymore, I held out hope that she would help me like I helped her the night her parents fought. This time, I felt like I had no one else to turn to and really needed her. I called Leigh crying and told her what happened. The distance between the friendship I thought we had and the relationship we had now widened. When we were best friends, Leigh would have been furious at my mother and offered to do whatever it took to help me. She might have even sought some hilarious form of revenge, like planting a fart pillow under my mother's seat during a dinner party. All I wanted was ground-level support, if anything, out of respect for the friends we were before. But she sounded bored as if I were the one acting this time and issued a reluctant "I guess you can hide them here." A more mature person would have told her to stuff it. Instead, I stuffed my journal under my shirt and ran down the trail.

Since we hadn't been running back and forth anymore, the brush had twisted across the clearing, leaving a web of sticker bushes. When I got down to the back sliding door, it was locked. So I walked around to the front and found myself at the door again, a stranger, not the girl who used to go everywhere with the Bentons.

This time, Leigh cracked the door open, grabbed my journal as if it were a huge inconvenience, said, "I've gotta go," and pulled the door shut so lightly, only a puff of air escaped. I stood there in silence wondering if we were ever really friends at all. It all seemed so fake, like a dream. Was I a convenient babysitting option for the Bentons all along? Did I become too entertaining for her friend Nickie and upstage her somehow? Or was it just fun for Leigh to bat me around like a cat plays with a mouse before cutting its life short? Did she just use me the whole time, thinking of me as a loser or just another one of her gawking child fans? Even now, the situation still haunts me, almost on the same level as a painful break-up when two people's truths will never align and differences stay suspended - permanently unreconciled.

Instead of heading back through the trail, I walked the long way home, winding my way up her driveway and out on the main road. It occurred to me that I had never walked that way before, mainly, because I didn't have to. This time, scraping up my legs on the sticker bushes didn't seem worth it. When I walked by Allison Frishy's house, the impact movie star Leigh had on the neighborhood became clear.

Before the Bentons came, everyone's world stayed focused on the Millwood – school, country clubs, and Izod shirts. Leigh not only showed everyone that possibilities existed beyond Izod, but that they were attainable. Suddenly, becoming a movie star, or in Allison Frishy's case, an Olympic gymnast, was more of a possibility than a distant dream. The realization bred frustration as parents like the Frishys refused to hire a private coach for Alison, stopping her Olympic dreams short. My aspirations were less clear to me at that point. I started out as a star-struck, spying little girl, but had truly cared about Leigh. It felt as solemn as the time I fed my parakeet too much lettuce, and it died. Walking home on smooth pavement instead of through barbed bushes held some hope. Even if our whole friendship was just an act for Leigh, I realized true friendships shouldn't be that hard.

The Bentons moved out as quietly as they moved in. No one in the neighborhood seemed to notice they were gone. And, despite my efforts to recover my journal from her mother and father in later years, I never saw Leigh or my journal again.

*"My mother busted me for driving on the wrong side of the road...
In my Big Wheel."*

11 . PRETEEN CRIMINAL CONFIDENTIAL

Without Leigh to bolster my confidence, my identity bobbled adrift, searching for a new friend to anchor me. For the moment, I parked myself at the Grayson's. Every spare minute, I hung out there to avoid my mother. Mrs. Grayson always made herself available, plunking down Pepperidge Farm Cookies and cups of Coke, then sitting down to talk about how I was doing and actually listening.

My love for Dave stayed intact, but my hopes for being picked as his official girlfriend got dashed to the ground as soon as he started dating Angela. Every time I'd watch them from my bedroom window, my stomach squeezed as he threw her over his shoulder like a sack of potatoes, then dropped her on a pile of leaves and pressed long kisses on her with her strawberry blonde hair sprayed all around. He still took me to get pizza and to the hardware store, but I knew my chances of becoming Mrs. Dave Grayson were over, unless I woke up one day looking like Stevie Nicks.

Before Peter left to work at night, he pulled me close on the sofa, putting his arm around me and telling me how much better off not having a friend like Leigh. He scratched my back, then let me knead his back because it was sore from hanging drywall all day. I still wanted Dave to touch me like that, but Peter was a substitute in a big brother kind of way. It felt soothing to hear him cut down Leigh for being such a bad friend and take up for me, completely different than my brothers, who constantly berated me – not in a fun brotherly way, but in a cruel, kill-your-pets kind of way, no doubt applauded by my mother. Being at the Grayson's and having that kind of support felt like that was my real home. If I could have moved in permanently, I would have. When the school year started, the Graysons were probably as relieved as I was and eager to see me dive into records, boys, and makeup like other seventh grade girls.

Since I was leaving elementary school and reporting to Addison Junior High, my nerves were especially jumpy not knowing what was hot in school supplies. When we walked out of the stationery store with new binders and clicky pens, two guys smoking in the parking lot said: "Oh look at the little kiddies, getting ready for school." Then, my mother fired back: "Yeah, well at least they're going to make something of themselves, unlike you- two losers hanging out in a parking lot." All three of us kids just looked at each other, jaws gaping in shock. We had never heard her take up for us, much less say something positive.

Addison Junior High spanned about five blocks and looked like any other government building stripped of any architectural detail. When the bus pulled up to the breezeway, the students tumbling out of the buses reminded me of the time I pushed a button on a vending machine and every single row emptied, leaving a log jam of chip bags, chocolate bars, and candy packages all trying to fit through the dispenser slot. Maybe I could get lost, become popular, or squeeze through the dispenser slot like everyone else. For now, I got in line with all the other kids and funneled in through the front door, deciding I would just do what everyone else is doing and try to fit in.

The school population had grown, so our seventh grade class reported to a trailer outside. It seemed like a private retreat out there, away from the sea of kids in the halls. The first thing I noticed about our seventh grade teacher, Mr. Hagwood, was his penchant for writing everything with a metallic, ultra-thin illustration pen. Thin black lines looked clean and sophisticated when he spelled my name, dropping the "e" and making the word "Jacki" alluring and mysterious. Without realizing it, the small act of misspelling my name gave me the confidence I needed to take one step toward claiming my individualism, not to mention, the ammunition to really set my mother off.

"You can't do that. Your name is J-A-C-K-I-E," my mother exploded. The angrier she got, the more excited I became, running outside to sing my name like Bingo: "J-A-C-K-I...J-A-C-K-I...J-A-C-K-I...Jack-I is my name, I." She threw the window open in the kitchen and yelled: "Shut the hell up. That's enough." Score,

I thought, realizing that being happy really upset her.

With my new name spelling and new best friend, Jenny, things started looking up as I joined the ranks of teenager-hood. Her dad slicked his hair back like Elvis, and her mom actually liked having us around. When they dropped me off at home, a Sunday drive excursion compared to their other commutes, her parents gasped at the size of our house. I didn't know whether to be proud or embarrassed, so I settled on confused. I would have picked their neighborhood where swarms of kids roamed the sidewalks. Jenny and I filled our time singing "Grease" and Linda Ronstadt songs and going to the mall, which became a competitive sport.

Reporting back to the classroom on Mondays, a swarm of girls clustered around the class queen bee, Mandy. One by one, she pulled merchandise she had gotten over the weekend out of her kelly green purse: new mascara, hoop earrings, and Cover Girl compacts. We thought her parents were rich and just gave her everything, until she leaned across the aisle and said, "I didn't pay for it."

"For real?" Jenny said.

"I just took it. We all do it," Mandy said nonchalantly. Green fabric and wooden handles that opened like a mouth made Mandy's purse look like an overweight frog when she stuffed the loot back in. Mandy founded her own shoplifting sorority, assembling on Mondays to review what they hocked over the weekend. "So, are you up for it?" Mandy asked.

Jenny recoiled; I jumped. The lure of being cool and accepted into Mandy's group while defying my police officer mother was too much to resist. Of course, the consequences of getting caught and the fact that I knew stealing was wrong never entered my mind once – only the promise of being cool. With nothing to hold onto or call my own, even my own personality, I was desperate to do anything to fit in. If the in thing to do included running over puppies, I would have followed that direction, too.

That weekend, Jenny's mom deposited us at King's Crossing Mall. But Jenny stood inside the mall doors, still debating whether or not to try it.

"Maybe if it's something you really, really want. Then, we'll try it," Jenny said.

"Okay."

We wove in and out of stores for hours not seeing anything "shoplifting worthy," until we found a jewelry store. That's where I spotted them- sparkling crystal cube earrings dangling on a metal spinning rack sitting right on the counter. Surrounded by shoppers, the clerk never saw me casually lift them off the rack. I studied them, held them up to my ear, then closed my hand so tightly around them, the posts stabbed the inside of my hand. Drenched in sweat with my chest on fire, I walked out of the store.

"See anything?" Jenny said happily.

"Nope," I surprised myself at how natural I sounded. "Let's go." We casually walked out of the middle of the mall and sat on a bench.

"Jenny, I just did it." I uncurled my hand and the violet felt holding the earrings was stained deep purple where my hands sweat so badly.

"Oh my God. I can't believe you did it. Now I have to do it," she said reluctantly. I took the earrings off and tossed the backing in the trash. Then, I stuffed the earrings in my down jacket. We continued paying for Christmas gifts. Then, Jenny nervously pocketed a glass tube of bubble gum Bonnie Bell lip gloss from the drug store. I didn't even notice she did it.

On Monday, Jenny and I joined the cluster of girls around Mandy and showed our prizes. "Is that all you got?" Mandy snorted, then revealed two fistfuls of items, making it clear that we were only semi-cool and clearly had some shoplifting to do. Nick, who sat in front of Mandy, leaned back in his chair, "Don't you know you guys could get in a lot of trouble?" His pale face filled in bright red as he shook his head in disapproval. No one knew I had a secret crush on Nick; I let my deep embarrassment and shame sink in, but it still wasn't enough to stop me from my mission to be cool.

We continued shoplifting and showing our prizes on Mondays. Then one Sunday, I got the ultimate opportunity: go shopping with the queen bee Mandy herself. Dad dropped me off at Mandy's house on his way to the Classic Car Club Christmas Party. This would be the first year I haven't gone. Last year, I handed out toys as the Christmas Elf; this year, pocketing toys as the Christmas Thief.

The shopping started at Huntington Mall. Watching Mandy work, I was amazed at her speed and efficiency as she effortlessly pocketed mass quantities of merchandise, turning her thin green frog of a purse into an engorged frog with an eating disorder. When she suspected someone was suspecting her, she paid. I couldn't keep up. By the time we were to be picked up at Huntington Drug Mart by her mother, I realized I hadn't pilfered any items to elevate my "cool" status in the group. While Mandy made her way to the make-up department, sliding two Cover Girl compacts in her jacket and a Max Factor mascara, the pressure to deliver mounted.

As I lingered in the candy aisle and considered taking a pack of Big Red gum, I noticed an older man with a tweed cap and glasses slid down his nose studying a label on a jar of vitamins near me. Something about that man just wasn't right, so I moved away from him and joined Mandy in the cosmetics aisle. Feeling the pressure of my shoplifting deadline, I looked down and considered replacing my about-to-run-out Bonnie Bell clear lipstick with a brand new one. The red, white, and blue tubes were loose in a plastic box. So I reached down and selected one and slid it into my jeans pocket when a flash of silver exploded in my face. The man with the tweed cap was holding a badge.

"You know what you did, don't you?" I shook my head yes. My throat squeezed so hard, I couldn't breath. Just then Mandy walked over, eyes as wide as Bambi.

"What about you? Were you shoplifting, too?" he asked her.

"No," she said, shaking her head back and forth in mock disbelief.

"I don't believe you. Was she?" he asked me. Afraid of not being cool anymore, I said no.

He walked us past the diaper aisle and through a freezing hallway made up of painted cinder blocks to a dark office in the back. He called in a check-out lady, who searched me and placed everything I had on a table.

"Did you steal this?" he said, holding up my almost-gone Bonnie Bell lipstick.

"No, that's mine," I said desperately, starting to realize the consequences of my actions.

"She's been working all day. Do you think she wants to be here dealing with you? A criminal," he barked at me.

"No," I squeaked.

"What about this?" He dangled a necklace in front of me.

"I bought that," I lied.

"Where's the receipt?"

"We threw all the receipts away and put everything in one bag."

"Okay, let the record state the subject had $23 in cash on her." As he started calling my parents, I slid down the wall, sobbing. The world as I knew it was about to end. My mother was going to kill me. Mandy just stood there looking as innocent a porcelain-faced angel.

"I'm going to get killed," I tell the detective. "My mother is a police officer." The phone dropped off his ear and he just looked at me.

"What? What county?"

"Ball." When he couldn't get my father at home, he called the Ball County dispatch. After explaining the situation, he hung up and announced, "Your mother's on her way." Then, they both left.

Mandy tilted her froggy purse upside down in the trash can and made it choke out everything she stole- heart-shaped stone earrings, dangly bracelets, and package after package of make-up. I secretly hoped they find them when they emptied the trash and call her and her parents back into the store. But that never happened.

A half-hour passed before I heard my mother's steel-toe police shoes pounding down the concrete hallway, then the office door blasted open. She was on duty, in full uniform with handgun, badge, and police blue enamel rectangle pin boasting: "Sharpshooter" when she got the news.

"Since she's only 12, I'm not going to process a record," the detective said.

"Thanks, Jim. I really apologize for this," then she growled in my ear, "I'll deal with you when we get home." There wouldn't be just screaming this time; I knew I was dead. She shoved me through the store holding my arm behind my back like any other criminal. Meanwhile, our entire neighborhood just happened to be standing in line watching the whole thing. Mr. Palio, whose kids I babysat, gawked at us. Mr. Dailey, whose kids I also babysat, stood in the Express Line staring at me. Her Ball County Police cruiser was parked out front in full view of the check-out line. She opened the back door and shoved me in while apologizing to Mandy that I embarrassed her and "put her through this." Marching your kid through a store with all the neighbors watching had to be one of the most embarrassing moments of her life, and she was about to make me pay dearly for it.

Before she threw the cruiser into drive, she threw a metal book of laws at me from the driver's seat, which nailed me in the chest. "Open to page 219. What does it say?"

"Drugs."

"Is that what you'll do next?" Already tried it, I thought, somehow proud of myself in a twisted way that I had a head start on her for once. "I'm sorry Jacki made you go through this, Mandy," she kept apologizing to Mandy, making me seethe. I can't believe she automatically assumed Mandy did nothing wrong and that it was all me. It shouldn't have been surprising. Whenever my friend's parents dropped me off, my mother said, "Thanks for putting up with her," as if I were such a colossal pain, then she'd slam their car door before they answered, "But she wasn't any trouble."

When we pulled up to Mandy's house in the police cruiser, Mrs. Simon turned powder white. But when my mother explained how everything was my fault and Mandy did nothing wrong, Mrs. Simon flatly said, "I doubt that," shooting Mandy a steely look.

From Mandy's house, my mother drove me straight to Ball County Police Headquarters, to acquaint me with jail cells and teach me a lesson. As her co-workers watched, she shoved me into the cell, a tiled room that looked more like the showers at Addison, except for the sliding bars. "This is what it's like. This is what you deserve," she said as she locked me in. Soon, another criminal arrived, so they took me out. "Now you know how it feels," she said, leading me out by the arm. I knew how it felt alright, after being treated like a criminal my entire life. This time, I felt like I deserved to be in jail for stealing and hated myself for being so stupid.

As she led me through the station, she had fun introducing me as: "my daughter, the criminal," "the shoplifter," or "the thief." I was horrified; she seemed alarmingly proud. When my dad found out, he broke down in tears. Then, he told me he was just telling his partner the other day how he never had to worry about me. I was a good kid. The possibility that now even my dad thought I was bad too was enough to make me want to die right there. The belief that I really was a bad person felt like spilling black ink on my favorite snow white sweater. With that kind of permanent mark, the sweater would never draw compliments again, and the joy of wearing it was ruined forever.

All night, my parents kept me up asking me why. After being talked to and screamed at, I didn't have the energy to endure another lecture. So I didn't tell them the truth that I did it just to be cool.

Two days later, my mother enrolled me in a weekly kleptomaniac clinic for juveniles. She drove me to the meetings in Ball County in what looked like a farm silo converted to a meeting space. When I climbed up the spiral stairs, I immediately noticed I was the only one not wearing a black concert t-shirt and flannel shirt, and all the other "juveniles" were between the ages of sixteen and twenty-one. At twelve, wearing an Izod polo, khakis, and Docksiders, I looked like a prep school girl late for sailing school. So I tried to cop an attitude, looking down to get hair in my face and kicking the carpet, only making myself trip, then getting shocked when I grabbed a chair to sit down. They laughed at me and said, "You're just a baby." I attended all the meetings, watching films about shoplifting and the cost to society, but I had already learned my lesson. I would never shoplift again. In fact, the incident started a slow transition from criminal to a hyper-law-abiding-citizen so afraid of getting busted, I feed meters on Sundays. Just in case.

Weeks after I "graduated" from juvenile shoplifting school, my mother hosted a spaghetti dinner for her Ball County Police friends. As I sat on the fireplace hearth, joking with the officers, one of them said, "Wait a minute, you're Jacki?" Spaghetti dangled off of forks as they all waited for my response. "That's me," I said. When they all looked around at each other in silence, I could only imagine how my mother painted me as her "convict daughter," rather than a misguided girl desperately in need of direction. Just knowing that I wasn't who they thought I was fueled my resolution that I could transcend everything my mother said about me.

Mandy continued shoplifting, but never got caught. Mrs. Simon still suspected Mandy after finding things all over her room that she has stolen. "Where did you get this, Mandy? And where did you get this? And what about this? You'd better not be lying to me because if I find out...." Mandy lied that she bought it, borrowed it or, "Oh, Susan must have left it here." The minute Jenny heard about my getting caught, she stopped for good. And so did I.

> *"I see a lot of guys...*
> *I just don't date any of them."*

12 . SEX PARTY

Summer in Millwood promised boredom as heavy as the humidity, until Dad started dropping me off at Tidwell Pool on his way to work. My obsession with slicing into the crystal water in the deep end without making a splash saved me. All day long, I threw dives over and over, springing off the low board because I loved the control instead of soaring off the high board and taking advantage of the time difference before you hit the water. Inwards, one-and-a-halfs, and front layout flips were my favorites. Other girls at Tidwell threw way more exotic dives than I did. You could see them arcing high over the pool from the gravel road coming in, then dripping wet and discussing their dives with coaches. Any dives I knew I taught myself. My "coach" was the drain at the bottom of twelve feet. Hitting the drain with my hands meant I had just executed a clean dive without making a splash.

Summer at Tidwell was like a tropical version of the Addison Junior High cafeteria. Steps led down to a huge patio area, divided cleanly into "freaks" and "prep" areas. Little kids and their parents stayed over in the kiddie pool area while Addison kids ruled the patio. The freaks pushed the picnic tables into the corner of the patio, creating a kind of back-of-the-bus scenario. Led Zeppelin "Houses of the Holy" blared from their boom boxes, and they shared their smokes while tanning in cut offs. Meanwhile, the "preps" shared *Seventeen* magazines while sipping smoothies from the snack bar and sunning in tropical-print swim suits. Since I didn't fit cleanly in either group, I sat in the middle. That's where I met Darla Harms.

One look at her intense green eyes jolted me with pure fear. That first impression was dead right. Not yet having learned the value of heeding instincts, I grabbed on to the best part about Darla Harms – proximity. She lived not quite walking distance, but close enough that my parents didn't hesitate to drive me down the hill to her house. Her puffy lips made her look like she pouted a lot. She zig-zagged when she walked, yet still managed to move in a straight line. And she was dangerously funny. With two mischievous senses of humor, we sat around laughing most of the time.

Just like Leigh and I, Darla and I did everything together. And just like Leigh, no one paid attention to what we were up to, not even my mother. When Darla's sister threw parties for her Redbrook High School friends, we crouched down low, swiped their tape of The Cars, and drank so much beer, we got bed spins and slapped our hands on the wall for support. By the time school started, Darla and I had become best friends.

When I boarded the bus for school, I noticed Darla sitting in the back with the freaks. So that was where I went. A new house had been built on our street, so now two new public school kids lived on our private drive, which gave me hope for having friends around, if not dreams of outnumbering the private school snobs. Priscilla, the new neighbor girl, flipped her mane of black hair, boarded the bus, and headed straight back to sit with the freaks as if she already knew them.

On the weekends, Darla got me a job selling pumpkins at the McNeely Farm across the street from her father's hunting store. Making my own money and being able to buy my own Eagles albums gave me a taste of independence that made me the happiest I had ever been. So were my parents and the Graysons. When my parents planned to go on a ski trip for a weekend, they decided I was mature enough to stay by myself to watch the house while Bruce and Matt spent the weekend at Grandmom and Grandad Eberstarker's house. The minute Priscilla heard my parents would be gone, she announced that her parents would also be away, and we should have a party at her house. Just like shoplifting, my desire to be cool overwhelmed rational thinking - having a party was the perfect opportunity to gain popularity with the "in" crowd. Too bad I failed to realize most of the "in" crowd already had juvenile records.

The Friday before school, my parents dragged their luggage out to the car as I sat serenely at the kitchen table. Taking an: "I can't believe how you've grown" swallow, Dad put his hand on my shoulder with pride as if I had just graduated with honors and said, "Be good now." My mother walked past me and said nothing, then closed the door to leave. At the last minute, she threw it open again and yelled, "No sex parties." Hmm, what's a sex party? I wondered. In the next 24 hours, I would find out.

At the bus stop, Priscilla quickly voided the plan to have the party at her house because her sister, Natalie, had to take the SATs the next morning. When we boarded the bus, Priscilla made an on-bus announcement inviting everyone to the party at my house, sending a wave of terror, followed by excitement through me. "If you weren't popular before," she said in my ear as she rolled ruby gloss across her lips, "You will be now."

Priscilla was as self-assured as a girl with an army of prize-fighting brothers behind her, except she was the youngest of five sisters. Natalie was the only one left living at home, and she couldn't have cared less about Priscilla. Maybe Priscilla derived a certain cockiness from her father's occupation as a CIA agent. Maybe she thought of herself as exotic, powerful, and top-secret.

The minute she got to my house, she took control. Ripping a piece of loose leaf out of my binder, she mapped out where every lamp and knick-knack was placed like a bank robbery. Then, she wrapped each item in paper towels and stowed them safely out of sight. Thinking we were throwing a harmless party with a few girls, I talked Dave into buying us a case of beer. By the time seven rolled around, the party consisted of Darla, Priscilla, me, and the Redmond sisters from school, sitting around the kitchen table, tipping back cans of Budweiser and looking at each other. One of Priscilla's friends who was old enough to drive showed up. Then Priscilla stood up and said, "This is boring. I'm going to get some people." I just kept drinking until the Budweiser bubbles no longer burned the back of my throat.

Thirty minutes later, Priscilla showed up with so many people, I got tired of answering the doorbell and taped a "Come in" note on the front door. Priscilla had gone to Arby's and made yet another announcement to all the fine twenty-two-year-old men hanging out there on a Friday night. Soon our front yard was buzzing like a demolition derby, as all the cars carved figure 8's into my father's meticulously manicured lawn. Then, the freaks from Addison showed up. Cece "Little Toke" Flyn and Heather "Cracky the Crab" Connally walked in, with roach clips made out of feathers fluttering off their denim jackets.

Known as the biggest potheads at Addison, they seemed to be respected for achieving high levels of partying unheard of for eighth graders. Cece thought it was funny that she partied so much, she stunted her growth. Meanwhile, Heather sported a party reputation as a "serious pothead," despite the uncool fact that she strapped on a giant red felt crab suit as "Cracky the Crab" and performed at little kid birthday parties for her father's Chesapeake Party Express company. And, there were guys everywhere. Guys who cleared junior high school ages ago. How they could have shown up, seen a bunch of us prepubescent Stevie Nicks wanna-bes, and thought: "Score," I'll never know.

Priscilla quickly hooked up with a broad-shouldered guy and announced they were taking her parents' BMW to "hunt for bears," except Priscilla wasn't old enough to drive. As I looked around, people were making out like crazy, trying to cook beers in the microwave, and rifling through my father's liquor cabinet. No connection existed that this was my house, and this entire situation was dead wrong. I watched it all from above my body, powerless to stop it. Sounds became muted as if my ears were cupped. Everything around me looked grainy, like trying to watch a movie in a smoke-filled theatre. Then, I thought about Dave. Now, he would take me seriously.

"Hey," I heard someone say as sounds seeped back into my ears. A tall guy with dark hair and a moustache stood there, considering me like I were a poster for a movie he was thinking about seeing. "What are you doing standing there all by yourself?" he said. Being with someone older than Dave seemed like a pretty good idea, like practice. When I looked around, there was Darla making out, Priscilla making out, and Cece making out. Just then, he turned my face back to him and leaned into me, kissing me full on the mouth. The only make-out experience I had to draw from was sixth grade when Chuck Sherba sucked my mouth so hard, he gave me a fat lip. I likened this kissing sequence to having a warm hot dog in my mouth. I didn't even know his name.

He lifted me up, carried me over to the sofa, and put me on his lap, still kissing me. Soon his hands moved like waves under my shirt. But I never felt them. Instead, I floated away from my body again, vaguely aware of what he was doing. Somewhere during this romantic interlude, I got bored. So I closed my eyes, got spins like at Darla's, and pretended to go to sleep. My memory to this day is that he carried me up to my room, put me on my bed, and left.

When I thought he was gone and heard people in my parents' and brothers' rooms, I sat up. When I walked to the door, I saw Dave walking down the hallway. I was thrilled he came to my party, until I realized he was only there to break it up. "Okay, everybody out," Dave boomed. "Let's go, party's over people. Get out." As fast as the Arby's crowd showed up, they left. Only Priscilla, Darla, the Redmond sisters, Cece, and Cracky stayed. We left all the beer cans, trash, and shredded lawn alone for the night.

The next morning, I realized my room had been ravaged. Cece and Cracky had asked me for bags the night before, but I idiotically thought they wanted to put their own clothes in the bag, not clean out my entire room. Discovering every empty drawer, every empty jewelry box, and the worst, the ripped up remains of the birthday gift I had handmade Dave felt as nauseating as the time my mother read my diary. The last thing I could bring myself to do was generate any kind of reaction other than disconnected shock and the sadness of realizing that after shoplifting and having an unauthorized party, I deserved all of my favorite things to be stolen. When I got down the stairs, the rest of the girls were packing up to go home. With the house trashed, the girls couldn't leave me alone with the aftermath fast enough.

"Later," Priscilla said as she coolly headed home. Outrage was what I should have felt, but emptiness left me no storage of emotion to tap into. Five minutes later, she showed back up because her sister had locked her out. That was the one and only reason she helped me clean. Darla, Priscilla, and I cleaned the house, then followed Priscilla's plan and replaced everything. Dave helped me ditch the empty telltale beer cans. But nothing could erase the lawn.

After Priscilla left and Darla's father picked her up, Dave came over. "My dad told me to come over here and get you. You're spending the rest of the weekend with us." He looked around the house sadly, "Man, Jacki. Who were those people?"

"I don't know," I said, as he sat down while I made an omelet.

"We have to talk," Dave said. When he locked his sapphire blue eyes on me and sat down without making a joke, I realized he was serious.

"I know," I said, feeling the weight of what would happen when my parents got home. This was the first time I felt like Dave really cared about me more than "little girl next door." The situation moved into dangerous territory when I asked him to buy that beer. I cut the omelet in half and slid it to him. In my preteen fantasy world, I felt proud that the omelet kept its shape and wondered what it would be like to be married to him and make omelets everyday.

"This is great," Dave said. "You're a good cook, you know that?" I turned to the refrigerator to hide my smile and stuck my head near the icemaker long enough to regain my composure to the task at hand: avoiding death.

"Dave, what am I going to say?"

"We need to work it out, okay? Especially about the beer," he said, setting his fork down.

"I know." I felt something change in me. He was taking me seriously now, except the wrong kind of serious.

"Jacki, I could go to jail for that you know."

"You're not going to get in trouble for this, I am," I said, suddenly feeling older and older. And again, accepting more responsibility in protecting an adult than I should. I had been making a career out of protecting my father from my mother without even realizing it. And this time, Dave. Meanwhile, I was out there all on my own.

"Look Dave, we hustle beer and wine all the time from people," I said. It was true. Since the drinking age was still under twenty-one, it was easy to "hustle" alcohol, which meant standing outside the liquor store and paying someone to buy you Boonesfarm. "I can tell them that's what I did, and that takes you out of the picture." I could tell I impressed him. His fork froze with a wedge of omelet oozing cheddar out of it as he just looked at me.

"You'd do that? Wow, and here I thought you were just the nice little girl next door," he leaned back, disturbed.

"That's what I'm going to say," I said, reassuring him that I would stick to my story.

"Okay, then," he reached across the table and touched my hand. My stomach flipped like the first time I threw a one-and-a-half dive. We bonded for a split second, then mapped out a plan that placed all the responsibility squarely on me. After all the times my mother had blamed me for my brothers' actions, the load seemed more comfortable than wrong. Dave helped me seed the gaping wounds in the front lawn, but it was no use. Neighbors from Bridlepath drove their cars slowly up our private, dead-end road, gawking and trying to figure out what happened there. Apparently, the entire neighborhood heard the cars racing on our yard.

Saturday night, I spent the night at the Grayson's. Dave went out on a date with Angela, but the jealous squeeze that gripped my stomach didn't happen. He touched my hand, and I knew he really cared about me. So I didn't care about his date for once. While he was gone, I got to experience life as a pseudo-Grayson, eating Kraft Macaroni and Cheese, a meat, and Matzoh crackers with sharp cheddar cheese. They ate the same exact meal every night. After dinner, I sat with Mr. Grayson as he watched *The Muppet Show, The Mary Tyler Moore Show,* and *MASH* while sipping scotch. Suddenly, he switched the TV off and turned to me, scaring the pants off me. That was probably the first time that television had ever been turned off.

"You know I think the world of you, Jacki," Mr. Grayson said in a deep, caring voice I had never heard before. Usually, everything he said sounded gruff. "Your mother's going to kill you. But we're still here for you, no matter what she does. We're going to help you."

"Will you adopt me?" my voice cracked and sounded as pathetic as Little Orphan Annie. He laughed, then slugged me in the arm, a practice he continued every time I saw him.

"We love you. You're a good kid," he said warmly, then back to his gruff, "Now turn my damn TV back on." I wrapped his words around me like a blanket.

His kindness supplied rich soil reserved for the seeds of other kind words. I'd drop the seeds there and ignore them. It would take years before they would grow. I was just lucky enough to covet those words and remember them.

Sunday, I shuddered as each number on the Grayson's digital oven clock flipped its metal feathers around like a tiny tin bird, announcing my impending doom. When my parents pulled into the driveway, Mrs. G walked me over to my house, and we all sat down at the kitchen table. My parents eyeballed each other suspiciously across the table. Mrs. G leaned toward them and said, "Jacki and her friends had a little party while you were gone this weekend, and things got a little out of hand." Mrs. G gave them a reassuring "but everything's okay" smile, but it didn't work. My mother sat politely, but her face quivered like a teakettle about to blow.

While Mrs. G stayed, things were very easy. Too easy. Very businesslike. I got grounded. Dad went outside with a flashlight to survey the damage on the lawn. Mrs. G said goodnight and "Go easy on her, she's a good kid." My fate should have been folded up and sealed, ending right there with a grounding. But as soon as Mrs. G shut the front door, the fury started.

"You. Sit," my mother spat. Then, she slapped a pad of paper in front of me. "I want the name of every single person who was here. Now." I just stared at her, hoping to serve out my grounded time and have this whole situation melt away, or at least, stay at a reasonable proportion. But the situation would grow way beyond the realm of kids throwing an unsupervised party. Giving up their names meant my new friends would turn to instant enemies. "Do it," she blasted me in the face, so I started writing. Meanwhile, Bruce and Matt ran upstairs to inspect their rooms, sounding like Goldilocks and the Three Bears, whining, "Someone's been sleeping in my bed. Ew, it feels all sandy."

"Oh, you let them spend the night at my house, did you?" my mother said with a "this will cost you more" growl. I wrote all the girls' names down because I didn't know any of the Arby's crowd, and my mother promptly snatched the list away. "Now get your ass upstairs. You're grounded for the rest of the year. And by the way, you have no rights." What else is new? I thought.

I went to bed as ordered. Just as I fell asleep, my door blasted open and my mother's fingernails dig into my pajamas as she hurled me against the wall. "You didn't tell me the whole story. I called every one of their parents, you little slut. Now get your ass downstairs right now," she yelled, punctuating every word by slamming my head against that damn Nutone speaker. When I reached the bottom of the stairs, I froze. A Baltimore County Police Officer sat at the kitchen table, quietly tapping a pen on his metal pad.

He watched me over the top of his metal-rimmed glasses as I walked slowly around the table and tightened the neckline of my strawberry-covered flannel nightgown, wondering what the hell happened. My parents sat dead quiet in the living room so they could eavesdrop while he questioned me.

"Hello, Jacki. I'm Officer Connelly. Heard you had a little party here this weekend. Why don't you tell me what happened," he said flatly.

"We had a party, and all these guys showed up. Priscilla went to Arby's and announced that there was a party," I said.

"Was there a sign on the front door inviting people in or anything?" he asked as he scribbled.

"Yes."

"We can't get 'em for trespassing," he said loud right to the living room door, so my mother could hear. "Tell me about your relationship with Troy Smith."

"Who?"

"Your friends told your mother you had sex with Mr. Smith at the party. Since Mr. Smith is twenty-four years old and you are a minor, that means he raped you."

"What? No." My heart jumped out of my chest and took my entire being with it.

"Why don't you tell me what happened." He leaned toward me, making the handcuffs on his belt jingle.

"But that never happened." I wanted to cry, but my body felt squeezed dry.

"Are you saying you don't remember? The girls said you passed out and he raped you."

"No, it's not true. He was kissing me, and I acted like I was asleep. He put me on my bed and left. That's it."

"Okay, I can understand if you don't want to talk about it. Your mother will have to get a statement from you then," he said to the door. "Were you aware jewelry was stolen?"

"What jewelry?"

"Your mother reported all of the family heirloom jewelry missing. Do you know who stole it?" he said as he positioned his pen on the paper, ready to record every name. My body caved in as I dropped my head on the table, thinking of all the jewelry my grandmother had given me and my mother. It was all my fault that the jewelry was gone. I couldn't bear upsetting my grandmother. She was one of the few people who really loved me. Because she raised me when I was little, I always considered her my real mother. This would hurt her most of all.

"Oh my God. I don't know."

After Officer Connelly left, my mother laid into me. "Your little friends told me everything. You only told me part of the story. I found out all about your little sex party. Those girls told me they saw him having sex with you, and don't worry, I'll get him. Tomorrow we're taking you to Bellview Clinic for a pregnancy test. Now, you're going to write down everything you did with him." She shoved another pad of paper at me.

"But nothing..."

"I don't give a shit if you have to sit here all night. You're not leaving this table until you right down everything that happened," she hissed as she shoved the pad of paper closer to me.

I slumped over the table for another two hours while my parents sat in silence in the den. Every half hour, she mumbled something to my father, who sat there motionless. Then, Dad walked in, eyes puffy from crying, head down.

"Just make something up, then go to bed or else you'll be here all night." The kitchen clock already said 2 a.m. So I wrote down three pages of what "supposedly" happened, using biological words like "breasts." But I refused to write down that he had sex with me, because he didn't. I slid the pad back to my mother, who quickly read it and exploded.

"You think I'm gonna believe you now after you lied to me?" Now the truth wasn't even good enough for her. "Go to bed. Tomorrow, you get the worst punishment of all- you're going to school."

> *"My mother found a seed in my room and sent it to the drug lab. Never mind the bird cage sitting there."*

13 . BUSTED

There was no escape. The reality of a space ship abducting me seemed far-fetched. But the trees swaying violently and scraping outside my window seemed a whole lot more likely to crash through the window, grab me with their bony branches, and toss me to the ground like an egg. I prayed for it. That way, I'd just be a pile of shattered goop at home instead of an egg ripe for splattering at school. I stared at their swaying shadows all night long, crying like a baby, until their gray trunks blurred solid black.

The next morning, I dragged myself out of bed like I did every day when I heard a soft knock on the door. Dad came in with his head down and sat on my bed, watching me smear eye shadow across my swollen eyelids.

"Oh honey," he said, touching my cheek. The torment he suffered was clear in his eyes, discs of soft hazel-olive suspended in a sky of bloodshot lightening.

"Guess I'm not the little girl you thought I was," I said. Just like with Dave, my age felt like it was rolling forward like an odometer in a speeding car. His shoulders caved inward as he sobbed. He put his hand on my head and hugged me, and I cried into his chest, leaving smudges of frosty eye shadow on his polo shirt.

"I don't know how to stop her," he said, shaking now. "She's out of control." Tears steamed up his glasses. When he looked up, he produced one of the cube-shaped handkerchiefs he always seemed to have in his pocket and dabbed at the puddle of make-up that had pooled under my chin.

"It's all my fault, Dad. Now I'm going to pay for it." It never occurred to me to ask him why couldn't he stop her himself, because he could have. One word from my father usually stopped her cold because it was as shocking as discovering a snail with teeth. But just like all the times we snuck out of the house to avoid her, he was one of us. He never fully realized the division that should have existed between parent and child, which was a screaming good time when we were out having fun, but brutal when you needed adult direction or support. I knew I was totally on my own.

Ready with a second layer of cover-up spread across my face, I made my way to the bus stop. Priscilla stood in the middle of the road and greeted me with, "Thanks a lot, you little bitch." She cocked her head to the side and said, "You got me in trouble. You're gonna be real popular now. Just like you wanted," she hissed, flicking my hair as I walked past her.

"She made me tell her who was there," I said sadly, trying to smooth my splayed hair back down.

"You think I give a shit? You should've lied, you idiot. Now I'm grounded, thanks to you." She shoved my shoulder. Lots of responses that included the word "fuck" filled my head, but my mouth stayed bound with an invisible gag. Incapable of connecting action and response, I failed to generate appropriate reactions almost constantly. Instead, my arms clung to my sides like a deflated punching bag. Day after day, my confidence squeaked weakly as I absorbed every jab, spitball, and insult hurled at me. Bitch. Slut. Whore. Loser. I collected the words like playing cards I held close to my chest so no one would see. But everyone did. Soon the words came from everywhere. The bus. The hallway. My mother. My brothers. And eventually, me. I started believing every word. Every morning, the words followed me off the bus, past the cafeteria, and into Mr. Hagwood's trailer.

"What's up Eberstringbean?" Mr. Hagwood said jokingly as he pulled a stool out for me at his desk. His smile dropped when he saw my bloated face. "Oh no. What happened?" I told him everything except the fictitious rape, and he shook his head in disbelief, first at my mother. "Jesus, it was just a party. Kids do stuff like this all the time. Your mother is a real piece of work," he said, considering his next words. Then, he took immense care convincing me this would all blow over and that I was most definitely not the loser here. But since he was my only friend, I couldn't believe him.

There was no surprise when Priscilla dropped me, but I thought Darla and I would stay friends and keep working at McNeely Farm together. Instead, Darla turned on me immediately, and Mrs. McNeely informed my father that I was no longer to report to work there and that they were "just shocked" after what Mr. Harms told them. So I lost my first job and my best friend. For my mother's next act, she would get a hold of the vice principal. So soon I would lose any respect I had earned from teachers.

In the middle of art class, I got paged to see Mr. Hinson, the vice principal. He shut the door behind my mother, and they left me outside as they met. Twenty minutes later, out came Mr. Hinson, a compact square of a man, with his face splotched red and his plaid polyester blazer crunched up around his neck. He looked as if he had survived an accident; my mother seemed gratified, as if she just pulled him from the wreckage. What the hell did she tell him, I wondered, clenching my teeth, a stress-inducing habit that caused massive migraines. The word spread through the faculty, drawing long stares and whispers as I walked by teachers in the hall. Officer Eberstarker was just getting warmed up.

Next, she pursued charges on the man who supposedly raped me, creating yet another chaotic scene when he showed up at our house demanding to talk to me. A fight ensued with my mother screaming, "You have no right to talk to her – she's a minor." Then, the guy returning with, "I'll sue you for defamation of character. You have no right to do this to me." His shoes scuffed the floor as my father blocked the front door and my mother called the police. "Oh yeah, well, now you'll have a record, you son of a bitch," she barked back over her shoulder.

An officer soon showed up and hauled the man away in cuffs while I curled into myself, trying not to throw up. Bruce and Matt sat with me upstairs in my dad's office, listening. Matt stayed silent, but Bruce capitalized on my misery as an opportunity to make me feel even worse. Even bully siblings know when they've crossed the line, but not Bruce. Now I didn't feel safe in my own house; going home became no different than riding the bus. My impatience at everyone around me preying on me had ignited an internal rage. Bruce chided me daily and soon convinced Matt to join in the fun. But when Matt happily informed me that my legs looked like "slut's legs," a plume of anger surged out of me so fiercely, I slapped him across the face. He never said another defamatory word to me again, unless he was talking about Republicans. I wish I could have mustered that response more often.

Meanwhile, my mother's plans steamed forward. Next, she surprised me at school with a lunch date at a statutory rape inquiry. She failed to make good on her promise to take me to a pregnancy clinic, yet was able to proceed with a statutory rape case despite physical evidence a rape kit would have provided – or not. Plus, no one had me identify a photo of the perpetrator. Since I didn't know his name, my mother could have been accusing Elmer Fudd of rape for all I knew.

She led me into a richly paneled boardroom as three sharp-looking women wearing business suits shook my hand. This time, they led her out of the room to a completely separate room where she could not correct, eavesdrop, demand, question, or collaborate like she did with Officer Connelly.

"Sounds like a wild party. Sorry I missed it," an attorney with dark straight hair spilled around her charcoal gray suit said. The other attorneys laughed. My shoulders fell down in relief. I liked them immediately. "So what really happened with this guy?" she said.

"We kissed, and he went to second base. That's it." I folded my arms nervously across my chest.

"So nothing really happened, did it?" another attorney asked as she looked over her tortoise shell glasses while paging through copies of the write-up I had handed in.

"No," I pleaded and prayed hope someone would finally believe me.

"Yeah, that's what we thought." The dark-haired attorney said. I wanted to crumple on the floor in relief right there. Finally someone believed me.

"So what's this about?" The woman with the glasses held the crinkled pages of what I wrote in the air as the relief I felt suddenly evaporated.

"My mother forced me to write something down, so I made it up. I mean if I got raped, wouldn't I be able to tell?"

"I should certainly hope so," the dark-haired attorney woman said, and they all laughed. I wanted them to be my sisters. Then, I wondered if any of them drove a Camaro.

"My mother refuses to believe that it didn't happen," I said, feeling relieved again at having someone accept the truth and actually listen to what I said.

"Well, we believe you." Oh, thank God. "There's not enough evidence here to pursue a case." Folders clamped closed, pen caps replaced, brief cases collected, and the whole thing ended right there. As far as I know, the case never made it to court. Although I obtained the police report, the juvenile court records from the '70s had been destroyed.

But just when I thought the party drama was over, my mother found another way to keep it going. Her next act: inviting all the party girls' parents over to our house for a meeting featuring the parental wisdom and street-smart warnings of Officer Eberstarker.

The night of the family meeting, the sky couldn't decide whether to splinter apart or harden into steel. The clouds froze into fractured wisps, motionless. On first inspection, our house looked as if we were inviting people in for a friendly neighborhood get together with chairs arranged in a circle in the living room, a rich coffee aroma wafting through the house, and tea cookies sitting primly on platters. My father politely took everyone's coats as they came in, except Mr. Harms, who refused to shed his dark wool coat.

One by one, the girls filed in and took a seat in one of our wildly uncomfortable Colonial dining room chairs. Heather "Cracky the Crab" Connally got dropped off without either parent. Cece "Little Toke" Flynn showed up with her mother, a frail woman who also had a flat, red, poc-marked face. The self-assured Priscilla Ladd arrived without either parent, while the Redmond sisters sat on either side of their steaming mother. Her anger was to be matched only by a visibly infuriated Mr. Harms, leaning back with his work boots planted in front of him and arms folded tightly across his chest.

Before my mother launched into her speech, I tried to picture everyone in his or her respective underwear, a technique I had learned from watching *The Brady Bunch*. Instead, my mind conjured up an image of Mr. Harms wearing only underwear and a blood-splattered apron, holding a carving knife and waiting to slice me paper thin, like he must do with the animals he hunts. Dave sat solemnly next to me as I slumped down and prepared to take full responsibility for every single thing that happened – again.

"My name is Pat Eberstarker, and I am a Ball County police officer. I'm here to warn you about where your daughters are heading, jail or teenage pregnancy." Then, she detailed the juvenile criminal process, something they were most likely intimately aware of. "I'm sure you've all heard what happened here. Cars were stolen and driven by girls not old enough to drive, underage drinking, and sex. We are still looking for the man who bought the beer, and I will press charges if I find out who he is," she said as Dave's body stiffened next to me. "The person responsible for all of this is Jacki." She left just enough of a pause to give everyone a chance to stare at me as if I were an exhibit.

My hands became fistfuls of sweat, yet I ached for Dave to hold my hand. Instead, I stared at the carpet and allowed myself to drift into a trance-like state, something I had become an expert at doing. As my mother talked, I floated out of my body up into a corner of the room, looking down at the faces…looking at me. The girls glared at me, hating me, blaming me. Their parents, clueless and more inconvenienced by this meeting than enlightened. On some level, my mother's words seared into me, but leaving my body provided anesthesia. The pain would surface much later, manifesting itself in the form of migraines, faulty choices, and self-abusive relationship selections.

"We're dealing with her," my mother said, glaring at me. "She has had all of her rights taken away, no TV, no friends, no phone calls. You need to control your daughters before they turn into delinquents like Jacki." The coffee maker gurgled and burped in the kitchen. My leg brushed Dave's. I took comfort that all of this would be over when I killed myself, until I saw my father, looking down at the carpet like Beaver Cleaver after he accidentally killed a robin with a slingshot. The disappointment that relief would not come at my hands made me sink further down into myself.

No one talked except my mother. After her speech, everyone left. Stacks of clean coffee cups and plates of tea cookies sat untouched. The borrowed banquet-size coffee pot had to be bench-pressed up off the counter and dumped out. The sky had made a decision, dispensing sheets of icy rain. On his way out our front door, Mr. Harms flipped his collar up against the rain, squinted his beady eyes at my father and said, "Good luck with her." At first, my father looked as if he was going to laugh; but instead, he looked Mr. Harms squarely in the eye and quietly shut the door.

> *"Sometimes I get heckled...*
> *By my inner child."*

14 . THE HECKLER COMEBACK

At a packed night at The Laff Lodge, I delivered the set-up: "I've been in therapy for over five years..." when a guy yelled out: "Go back! You need it!" making the audience roar. I stopped my set cold and fired back: "Can I have your phone number? Because you're just like every idiot I date," the audience went crazy cheering. The man never said another word. The comeback worked, but the damage was done. He had found me out and left a wound. Cutting myself down was like saying you're fat and hoping everyone around you says: "No you're not." When the heckler confirmed, yes, You are still messed up. You still do need therapy, sister, I felt as devastated as if I had accidentally exposed my breasts to the audience, and no one noticed.

Getting heckled was a comedy job hazard. If a heckler was particularly good, he could sabotage your whole set and steal the audience, making you look like a hack. Although I carried around a small arsenal of comebacks, like: "Do I get in your way when you're setting up tampon displays at Piggly Wiggly?", I never used them. Instead, comebacks fired out of my mouth like a bullet. A good comeback made the audience turn against the heckler. A great comeback forced the heckler under the table. Mine seemed to do both.

My success rate with hecklers could be attributed to being sabotaged my entire life by my mother, my brothers, and random kids on the street. I had not found success with comebacks then, once getting pelted with icy snowballs for a half hour after yelling: "Oh yeah, that hurt" at the bullies, while my brothers bolted home. As I got more experience being on stage and had decided I didn't care what the audience thought and was just there to have fun, people rarely heckled me. Maybe my false sense of confidence kept them quiet, or maybe the material was actually funny. Or perhaps the hecklers in the audience paled by comparison to my mother's criticism, my worst heckler of all time.

My mother's attempts to flatten every aspect of my life had always haunted and disturbed me. Several years before, I had set out to find out why after my traumatic eighth grade party, she manufactured a rape that never happened, then destroyed every single facet of my life: school, friends, work, and spirit. When Grandmom Wasser had died, I faced my mother for the first time in six years since my parents divorced. When my mother first saw me at the funeral home, her jaw dropped. It must have been a shock seeing a twenty-four-year-old woman, not the eighteen-year-old girl I was the last time I saw her.

"Hi Jacki," she said numbly. There were no hugs and she didn't get up from her chair. She just looked at me. Her hair was still bleached an oatmeal-colored hue and she wore a faded, rust-colored corduroy suit Mrs. Grayson handed down to us several years ago.

"Hi," I said. "Do you need me to do anything for the reception afterward like go to the liquor store or something?" All proper Catholic funerals featured a full bar.

"You can't buy alcohol. You're underage," she snapped.

"That's funny," I said, "Every weekend, I walk right up to the liquor store counter and the nice man sells me beer." My brothers cracked up behind me.

"How old are you?" she demanded.

"Twenty-four," I enunciated clearly, as a small dose of bratty sarcasm escaped from my mouth.

"Hhmf," she turned away and lit a cigarette.

Before the funeral, she called me to ask if I wanted anything from my grandmother's house. "Can I have the vacuum?" I asked. "No," she said bluntly, and that was that. Nothing had changed – I should have told her I didn't want the vacuum under any circumstances, and she would have delivered it to me herself with dirt still in the bag. At the time, I had resorted to wrapping my shoes with duct tape and walking around my apartment because I couldn't afford a vacuum cleaner. When it was time to relegate the will, my mother arranged to meet me with my inheritance, my grandmother's silver collection.

Months after the funeral, we arranged to meet in front of a Home Depot store outside of Baltimore. When I drove up, my mother and her husband stood waiting behind an older model Chevy pick-up truck with the tailgate flipped down. I immediately recognized her weathered flair-leg Faded Glory Jeans as another one of Mrs. Grayson's hand-me-downs. Her shoulders hunched forward as she stood there with her hands in her pockets. She looked so small to me then compared to the way I remembered her towering over me when I was little. It was like visiting elementary school and having to kneel to reach the water fountain, then remembering how tiny you once were. Her husband went milling around Home Depot and left us so we could talk. When I walked toward the tailgate, I noticed my grandmother's silver flatware poking out of a crumpled Giant Food paper bag with fat rubber bands wrapped around it.

"What did I do to you that was so horrible?" my mother asked in disbelief.

"Where should I start? You smacked the shit out of me when I was little, verbally abused me every chance you got, told me I was a piece of shit, fat ass, slut, stupid...want me to keep going?" The words soared right over her head as if I were talking about someone else.

"My mother told me I was shit, too," she said as if we were friends and she was empathizing with me. "She hated me because I wasn't a boy," sending a chill through me since Grandmom Wasser had told me my mother had tossed an IV bottle across the room when she found out she had just delivered a girl, not a boy. "I had a terrible childhood," she continued as sadness welled up in her eyes. I wondered how her childhood could have been so bad when she was clearly her mother's favorite who ultimately inherited my grandmother's house, money, and all of her possessions. "When we were growing up, my parents never allowed me any freedom. I married your father to get out of the house and had you kids before I was ready."

"You married him to get out of the house?" My stomach started to dance like a boxer's, I wanted to level her with a knock-down punch so badly.

"Being married to your father was no picnic, let me tell you," her familiar bitterness started to surface – wisps of smoke on oil. "He never stood up for me. And that attempt at a reconciliation when he took me on that vacation to Maine was a joke," she laughed as I stood there too stunned to speak. At least he tried, I wanted to yell at her, but my shoulders sunk down, as I felt so sorry for my dad. At the funeral, he walked straight over to her and her husband, kissed and hugged her, then shook her husband's hand. In that one moment, my respect for him reached skyscraper heights. I hoped I could absorb that level of class from him, put myself aside, and do the right thing one day. It was clear that in their marriage, he tried, she didn't. He gave, she took. It broke my heart that here he was, still giving.

"But why did you hate your own children?" The million-dollar question.

"I was in a bad marriage and did the best I could," she said as I stood there in disbelief: How could she possibly blame her marriage for that? Then, she unleashed her attitude. "You kids had it damn good. You got everything you ever wanted," she glared at me as if she wanted to hit me. It was true that my parents made sure we had the best Christmas and birthday presents. On our birthdays, she'd spend all day sculpting an elephant out of a cake, then smack us for allowing a piece of wrapping paper to drift to the floor. All holidays and birthdays were punctuated by one or more crying kids. As a result, permanent self-doubt sunk to the bottom of my mind, a cinder block embedded in the muck of a pond always there to remind me I really didn't deserve those gifts because I was a bad kid.

"We had everything we wanted, but rights. We were just objects to be seen and not heard," I said, repeating her exact words.

"Children have no rights until they are eighteen," she barked like a drill sergeant. "That's responsible parenting."

"I can't believe you think that." It became obvious to me at that point that she really couldn't see how anything she did was wrong. She assumed absolutely zero responsibility for her actions, yet she was proud of "how well we turned out." I stayed on target and asked her to clear up my mind about the worst thing that ever happened to me, the "sex party" in eighth grade.

"Why wouldn't you listen to me that I never got raped?" I plead to her and felt like we jetted back through time to the exact moment when she was out of control, calling the police and holding parent meetings.

She smirked before she answered, "The only person who 'got it' was that guy because now he has a criminal record for sexual assault," she said proudly as if she were a heroine who had dragged a serial murderer to justice all by herself. Yet, when I checked, I discovered no criminal record.

"How fair is that? Nothing happened." I couldn't believe what I was hearing.

She must have derived pleasure from fabricating the rape situation, exaggerating the party chaos, tearing me down, then acting as if she were saving me from the very situation she created in the first place. Maybe it was emotional Munchausen by Proxy, a way to gain sympathy and attention from colleagues about dealing with a delinquent child? Maybe she craved the attention of calling parents together and having the audacity to position herself as saving their children as she ground her own child to chalk in front of everyone? And after years of believing that those girls had made up the rape story to get me back for telling on them, I'm convinced my mother alone escalated the story from kissing a minor to raping a minor. Why else would a police officer parent not take her child to seek medical attention and a rape kit immediately? Why would the kids on the bus not make fun of me for the supposed "rape" they witnessed? Why were the other of-age men who pawed at the other minor girls not charged? No matter what her reasons, the choices she made were sick and dreadfully wrong, but they were still her choices.

"You were a minor. Sexual contact with an adult is against the law," she said as if she were charging a suspect before cuffing him.

"Did you ever think about what would happen to me when I went to school? About kids beating me up and terrorizing me on the bus everyday?" Suddenly, the pain from eighth grade surfaced again, and I felt like crying and pleading: How could you do that to me?

"I was trying to protect you," she said, leaning forward.

"What?" I said, genuinely shocked.

"But you can't see that, can you?" she said with deep resentment.

"You believed everyone else but me. You still do, even now." I was amazed at her self-righteousness, not to mention complete ignorance of how her actions impacted others.

When the conversation moved on, I tried to be fair, telling her I appreciated the ways I was like her. How I had the courage to go to Atlanta by myself and make my own life. How I handled myself and pursued after opportunities, like her. She seemed almost scared hearing me say positive words, maybe even proud. I wasn't sure. Her husband walked over from Home Depot with his head down like a horse humbly asking to be invited into a herd. We had lunch across the street and hugged when we parted ways. I felt slightly relieved, like some questions were answered, but nothing made sense. When I got home and told Dad and his wife, April, what happened, Dad was stunned. Maybe in retrieving answers for myself, I answered questions for him. April shook her head in disbelief.

"She's blaming everyone else for why she treated you the way she did," April said. I knew April was right, but it took me awhile to process what my mother said. Dad said it was cathartic for me to gather all this information, but warned, "Don't get obsessed with it." I didn't go see my mother to make her feel better; I did it for myself. That night, I dreamt my mother had locked me in a basement. Waking up with my jaw throbbing from gritting my teeth all night, I couldn't shake feeling like I had to escape. The more I thought about what she said and how she refused to accept responsibility for her actions, the more my anger bubbled to the surface. When my anger reached a rolling boil, I wrote her what I now call my "angry, self-righteous 20-something" letter:

"Dear Mom,

I'm glad I met with you because it cleared up a lot of things in my mind. But eventually, it made me furious. All I heard was how a bad marriage, unsupportive husband and miserable childhood made you do what you did to me. I also heard that you didn't understand exactly what you did. But I never heard you accept direct responsibility for your actions. That's not good enough for me. The most important thing I learned was your attitude that I had absolutely no rights as a human being until I was 18.

"I had absolutely no desire to stay in contact with you after you left. You always treated me like an object to be seen and not heard. An object that was frequently told it 'looked like shit,' was stupid, 'looked like a slut,' 'was running her mouth again,' and other negative comments that made me want to kill myself.

"I wasn't allowed any privacy because it was your house. I didn't deserve to have the shit smacked out of me after you read my diaries. That was none of your business. But since I had no rights, everything was your business. When I was little, I remember taking Bruce and trying to run away. I always wanted to run away from you. When I was older and self-destructive and suicidal, I felt like I was trying to break away from that trapped feeling. Now I know where that comes from and that has helped me.

"I also learned that you had a philosophy of raising children that entailed nipping in the bud problems that didn't exist. When your husband said you were proud of how we 'turned out,' I couldn't help but wonder why you never saw that we were good kids to begin with. I got in trouble because all I ever heard was how I better not do this or do that. I even did drugs before dinner to see if you would catch me. You never noticed. I am completely floored that you still, to this day, think I got raped. But I told you nothing happened. You believed everyone else. In court, finally someone believed me. Thank God one thing went in my favor.

"You created the chaos you thought you were protecting me from. But now you gloss over the incident and tell me you were trying to protect me. If you were, why did you go to my school, have a parent meeting and make me the school joke, school slut, school loser? You never even thought of what I went through every day and how I was making plans to kill myself.

"Please don't get the idea that I am blaming you for everything bad that ever happened to me. I want you to know your role in my childhood. I never had a mother in my life. I knew you as the enemy. Every day, all three of us ran to our rooms in terror as soon as we heard the garage door open. You would scream bloody murder the minute you walked through the door- if there was a sock on the floor, glass in the sink, magazine out of place. We never knew what would set you off, but something always did.

"It's sad that you had to take out everything bad that happened to you on your children. Right now, I can't accept invitations to spend holidays with you. I understand that you're trying, but I'm not convinced anything's changed other than you have finally accepted that I am a human being with rights. I now have a right to make choices, and I am choosing not to have the kind of relationship I think you want.

"I understand what happened to you as a child because the same thing happened to me. History has repeated itself. It's not your fault that you learned from bad examples. But knowing that, you need to take some responsibility for what happened. Dad has accepted his part in this. But even if he went back, he would do the same things all over again. It made me sick that you said you married him to get out of the house. It's sad, but I think he actually loved you. It's one thing to learn that I was a 'mistake,' but another to find out one of your parents didn't love the other one. Luckily, Dad tells me I'm 'the best mistake he ever made.' Or is it really true that you didn't love him? If he was only a way out for you, then my theory that we were just possessions and pawns to you must be correct.

"I have gained positive attributes from you- I don't let people run over me, I succeed in anything I set my mind to and I'm aggressive. I have made a great life for myself. Dad helped me get started, but I did everything else all by myself. I am truly happy you are happy in your life now. Please understand that I forgive you, but I don't think I want you in my life right now. – Jacki."

A month went by, then I received her response:

"Dear Jacki,

I was so delighted at our meeting- a productive first step to a reconciliation, I thought. Your letter brought to mind your great grandmother's adage: 'When they are little, they step on your feet. When they are grown, they walk on your heart!'

"You have managed to misconstrue a lot of what I said. You have a self-centered mindset with no thought or room for the feelings or motives of other people. I told you as you were growing up, there were no courses in child rearing- I did the best I could. Only when you have children of your own will you understand.

"You had a good family life– a nice home (your own room), good food, nice clothes, the best public schooling and parents that tried to make you feel loved and wanted. You had far more advantages than most children. Our home was not 'The Brady Bunch,' but it certainly was not the hellhole you describe either!

"You keep reiterating your 'rights!' A child has the right to food, clothing, shelter and responsible parenting (love and discipline).

"You keep referring to the fact that you were a good kid and could be trusted. Trust is something you earn. The shoplifting episode, illegal party and, by your own admission, the drug usage, do not constitute trustworthy behavior. I arrested teenagers for those offenses! A police officer's children cannot be above the law- they should be good examples to the community. I hope you never have to suffer the humiliation I have, due to your antics.

"If your mental health professional feels that venting your frustrations, anger and hostilities on your mother and shifting the blame are productive, then you had better find another counselor. I am certainly not perfect and have made mistakes, but I will not allow you to make me your 'scapegoat.'

"I have suffered greatly. I not only divorced a husband (I did not even ask for alimony), but I lost my children, home, friends and lifestyle. I felt that making you 'pawns of war,' as in the case in so many divorces, intolerable and inhumane.

I tried to raise you to be responsible and not domineer your life. I was ordered around my entire life, and I tried to allow you the freedom to make your own decisions. I was hoping that over the years, you would be wise and mature enough to see my side and accept my unselfish motives. I attempted to keep in contact with you, but you didn't want me! When I needed you, you were not there. I have always been here for you, and I always will be!

"Jacki, I love you and only want the best for you. I hope you are happy and successful in your endeavors - Mom."

Reading her letter was like riding a bike and inhaling a bug, then pedaling faster to forget you just swallowed a live insect. When I read: "I hope you never have to suffer the humiliation I have, due to your antics" sentence, I felt embarrassed for getting in trouble. It was embarrassing for everyone in the family, not just her. She will never see that she created an environment that invited that kind of behavior. She only taught us what not to do. When we did something positive, we were still met with criticism and scorn. So it was no wonder I got in trouble with the wrong crowd. Funny how she couldn't see how her antics of putting me on display at a parent meeting after the party caused me humiliation. I was most amazed that she expected me to accept all the responsibility as if I were a full-grown adult at the time.

After I read the letter a few more times, the bitterness lifted and revealed one truth: This was who my mother was. Something shifted with that simple truth – I now considered her my biological mother, not my enemy. Realizing she would never accept responsibility for any of her actions made the anger lift and indifference settle in. Not having a relationship with anyone who tore me down like a heckler was absolutely the right decision for me. At the same time, I felt gratified that I told her what I thought and didn't allow her to make excuses and gain access back into my life. I was ready to move on. So I folded up her letter, hid it from myself, and started surrounding myself with people who were nice to me. I mistakenly thought Aston was one of those people. But the truth that my boyfriend was about to become my second biggest heckler had not surfaced until the day I was preparing for a big comedy show.

"Comedy is more important to you than I am," he snapped, shoving my notebook aside as I read over my notes.

"What are you talking about?" I said, pulling my notebook into my chest to protect it.

"I don't want you in clubs hanging out with other guys. Comedians aren't respected, they're low-life strippers who hang out in clubs all night." It felt like getting punched in the gut.

"You're comparing me to a stripper? You've never even seen me perform," I said, devastated, instead of generating the appropriate reaction of anger. Performing stand-up felt empowering, like a sexually abused woman who strip dances to gain power over men. He was right, performing stand-up was a lot like stripping and baring your soul, except no bouncers stood by ready to protect me. Once I came off stage and complained to him about hecklers. Instead of soothing my nerves, he said: "You asked for it by putting yourself up there."

Instead of bowing out of the show, I defied his insults, dragged myself to the club, and performed anyway. Somehow I had gone against everything I had learned as a therapy connoisseur and found another life heckler. Instead of evacuating from the relationship immediately, I stayed in it, carrying the "postcard traumatic stress disorder" image of happier times when he was nice to me.

From then on, the highs of coming off stage dropped off sharply to devastating lows of depression. The mood rollercoaster started to wear on me, and my weight shed off of me again. I isolated myself, only to surface briefly if Aston felt like acting nice to me. Just as quickly, he pinned me down on the bed and tried to force me to pose nude so he could take pictures of me. I refused. Then, he offered to fix my childhood ten-speed bike I adored that my dad had shipped down to Atlanta for me. But instead of fixing it, he gave it away and presented me with a cheap mountain bike from Target. As I stood there feeling like a child who had just gotten her doll stolen, he berated me for being unappreciative. I had given him all the power to control me like a tattered little waif of a puppet. He filled the chaos hole that used to be filled by my mother, telling me stories of how much more accomplished his former girlfriend was at performing ballet for the Royal Ballet Theatre than I was at comedy. Eventually, he wore me down to a fine powder, then with one blow, blew me out of his life. Then, he was courteous enough to inform me he had met someone new and was "fucking her brains out."

At the same time, clubs started going under left and right. With drink minimums, a new genre of potty-mouthed, blue comics, and the arrival of stand-up comedy on cable, it's no wonder the local clubs went under. The Laff Lodge and Will Baty's went under on the same day. The only bonafide "A" club left in town was the Yuk it Up. Since the Yuk preferred to put male comics up on stage, I barely considered it an option. All of the comics shared their despair, even the rogue comics. It seemed like comedy itself was breaking up with me, and I was doomed. I hated my job, comedy started to evaporate in front of my eyes, effectively removing my chances of getting the life I wanted. Without Aston around to sabotage me, I would soon start doing it myself.

> *"I got grounded for so long,*
> *I earned interest."*

15 . THE "I HATE JACKI" SHOW

The junior high-grade abuse continued for months. I tried cutting myself down first before they had a chance to, but the freaks turned it against me, saying I was "proud to be a slut." But not once did any of them make fun of me for a rape they supposedly witnessed, a realization it would take years for me to uncover. Instead, they got their material from what I wore, how I walked, and what object my butt most closely resembled. Eventually, I gave up, stopped smiling and looking up when I walked.

Mrs. G was so upset seeing me like that, she took me out to get Cokes and French fries and gravy, a Baltimore tradition. Meanwhile, my mother seemed as content as someone who had managed to train her dog perfectly, getting it to bark on command and sit when ordered. While Mrs. G tried everything in her power to see me return to some state of happiness, my mother seemed to enjoy my diminished state of being. Mrs. G pleaded with me, saying she couldn't stand it that my mother "sucked the life out" of me. But it didn't matter. Mrs. G's kindness would go miles, but my depression quickly outran her efforts. No one could reach me. I hunched over so badly, the school nurse reported that I had scoliosis. At least I had scoliosis, I thought, because I had lost all of my friends, the good ones and the ones I never should have been friends with in the first place. Mr. Hagwood was my only friend.

But there was hope. When I got off the bus one day, Priscilla asked if I wanted to come over after school for UTZ potato chips, like we used to do before all this. I was completely shocked that she wanted to be my friend again, thinking maybe if I regained her friendship, people would just leave me alone. On the way over to her house, we cut through the woods and sat in the living room of a house still under construction overlooking the same spot where Leigh and I used to puff cigarettes.

"Wanna get high?" she said, pulling a baggie full of what I thought was pot out of her woven purse.

"Okay." She stuffed her metal bowl with pot and lit up. The air felt like frozen daggers tumbling down your throat when you breathed in, and the pot hit me fast, making my head feel oversized like a bobble doll. "Want another one?" she said.

"Sure," I said, trying to sound self-assured like her.

"Okay," she said in a reluctant tone like she didn't think I could handle it. I mistakenly decided to prove her wrong.

On our way back through the woods, I hallucinated, a brand-new terrifying experience for me. An angel with huge wings and a transparent prom dress floated through the trees and hovered in front of me, making me drop my L.L. Bean backpack. Shadows darted behind trees. A hairy black spider the size of a car squeezed our house. I couldn't tell whether I was asleep or awake. So, I grabbed Priscilla's arm, shaking it to see if she was really standing there.

"Get the hell off me," she swatted my hand.

"This is so weird. Is this a dream? Wait. I can't tell." I said, stopping repeatedly to ask her if she existed. "Are you really here? Wait." She threw her pocketbook over her shoulder and walked in front of me, making a tree branch snap in my face. When I got home, I was so terrified, I went straight home and slept.

Monday, Priscilla had all the material she needed to start a whole new "Hate Jacki" show, laughing at how easily I "fell for it." The whole thing was a set up. I started hating myself more for being so stupid. As they kept their show going at my expense, I thought about killing myself again. Using a gun seemed to be the most obvious technique. Because my mother was so paranoid that our house was being constantly cased, as if it were the Louvre, she kept loaded guns by her bed, in the drawers, and in the closet so she could quick draw on any intruder. I didn't want to leave a mess and could too easily visualize my father on his hands and knees cleaning up. Then it occurred to me that killing myself was exactly what my mother wanted. And, using her gun might give her satisfaction, as if she had pulled the trigger herself. I changed my strategy right there: guns were out; pills were in.

After school, I searched through my parent's medicine cabinet looking for prescriptions to kill myself with, but was completely disappointed when the only bottle I found contained salt tablets for contact lenses. Realizing that the only damage I might do to myself was high blood pressure, I thought of yet another plan. The window that faced the Grayson's house had a straight drop to the basement steps. If I dove head-first like at the pool and nailed the drain, just like at the bottom of Tidwell's twelve-foot deep well, I might die. I hung my head out the window for hours looking down at the blackened leaves piled up in the basement stairs, spitting to see if I could hit the drain, and fantasizing about the concrete rushing toward me, then darkness, and for once, peace. Then, I suddenly wished I had taken physics. Without a springboard, would I be able to slice the air straight down like I did at Tidwell Pool? What if I needed the extra exertion to succeed? What if it didn't work? I could end up paralyzed. The fog of questions ended when I heard a knock on my door. "Jack, come on down and get some popcorn," Dad said, sending the disappointment that I still have to live in all of this flooding back again. No matter what, I had to stay around for my dad. As a junior codependent in training, I knew I couldn't leave my dad, protecting him yet again but inadvertently saving my own life.

Out of nowhere, my parents issued a positive direction, and my mother suddenly wanted to be my friend. "We realize we expected you to carry too much responsibility," my mother said. "You were not old enough to stay alone, and that's our fault." My mouth dropped like a drawbridge at a miniature golf course. Finally, something was only 95 percent my fault. "Your job is not to watch the house. Your job is going to school. That's what you need to focus on."

"We're so amazed how all this has happened and your grades are still excellent. But we don't want to see your grades slip," Dad said, eyebrows up, a slight sign of pride.

"But we realize this has been tough on you, so we want to take you away for the weekend, just Mommy, Daddy, and you," my mother said sweetly in the voice she usually reserved for anyone but family. "We love you." She leaned over and hugged me, making me feel slightly appreciative for the reassurance, yet queasy like the first time I met Darla. My first instinct jolted me; but since she was being nice, I felt like maybe I should give her a chance. I longed for friends and thought maybe your family could be your friends, like on TV.

Since I felt so responsible for the jewelry being stolen and the lawn getting destroyed, the last thing I wanted them to do was spend money rewarding me with a ski trip. So I let the invitation to go skiing with my parents slip. But the direction that I should focus on being a student stayed. First, I ditched all black t-shirts, tossed my Led Zeppelin *Houses of the Holy* album, and any item with a feather on it. Then, I retrieved every stitch of preppy clothing out of my closet — pinks, greens, ducks, and seashell belt buckles.

With or without the safety of pink and green ducks, the freaks kept screaming at me. So I read Shakespeare to lock in my concentration and drown out their words. When I came home shaking off the day's quota of spitballs, my mother intercepted me and hugged me before I retreated to my room. This time, I took it in, letting my body slump and the tears flow. She said she wanted to help me "through all this," and I believed her. I wanted for her to love me and for me to love her, but it felt like trying to walk on a balance beam during an earthquake, knowing a jolt would eventually knock me off, just not knowing when.

To make things better for me, she bought me Clinique make-up in hues as unnoticeable as a wheat stalk, but the freaks still made fun of anyway. Then, she offered to transfer me to a private school. On some level, I relished the thought of fitting into the neighborhood with my very own private school sticker plastered on the back of the station wagon. With all of her efforts trying to pull herself up to a higher social class, I'm sure she did, too. After rounds of tests, interviews, and tours, I selected St. Stephen's Preparatory School, an all-girls Catholic school. When I bounced into Mr. Hagwood's to tell him the good news that it looks like I'll be transferring to St. Stephen's, he just stared at me, speechless. First period, he had me pulled out of class.

"Have a seat," he said as he slammed the door behind me. I felt scared that I did something wrong, like the time he thought I put a tampon in Jan Leavy's pencil case. He paced back and forth screaming at me for twenty minutes, then slumped over in defeat when Jenny fessed up.

I sat on the same stool I fidgeted on every morning as I hid in his classroom away from the freaks as he paced in front of me. "You can't transfer schools," he said, wringing his hands. I started to cry, and he slid a tissue box over to me. "They pick on you because they're losers. It was just a party. Kids do it all the time. Your mother has turned this into a federal offense." He kneeled down and faced me. "They're going to find out about you – then what will you do?" My blood cubed itself into ice. The thought hadn't occurred to me, but I knew he was right. There truly was no way out of this nightmare. I cried harder as he took a sip of coffee. "Look, you're so much smarter than these kids, and you're going to go places in your life. Plus, you have friends here. I'm your friend. You're a good girl, Eberstringbean." I laughed a little at my seventh grade nickname, then he walked over and held me, letting me press my tears into his wide-wale corduroy jacket.

I always loved Mr. Hagwood and wanted to be special to him. Now I knew I was. I blew my nose and reported back to class. Somehow deciding to stay at Addison felt like a huge relief. Staying in familiar territory seemed safer than treading on unfamiliar, private school terrain. When I got home from school and told my mother I was no longer interested in private school, she blew one irritated steady stream of smoke and said, "You're going to do whatever the hell you want anyway, Lady Jaquelyn." I thought she would be happy that I felt good about my decision to stick it out. But with her response, I couldn't help but wonder if she was more upset that she wouldn't get to plaster a private school sticker on the back of her car. Later, I would realize I was right, she was more concerned about pulling up her social status up and joining the private-school-sticker, station wagon-driving, fur-coat wearing neighbors than the well being of her kids.

By the middle of the year, instead of the ridicule slowing down from the sheer monotony of material, it intensified. Suddenly, notes started appearing in my locker courtesy of Darla Harms with motivational messages like: "Everyone hates you. Something terrible is going to you because you deserve it, and I'll be there laughing at your grave."

My frustration gelled with impatience and a timer went off inside my head: I'd had enough. So I met with Mr. Moore, the guidance counselor, explained the situation, and simply asked if I could ride another bus. When Mr. Moore asked why, I dropped a fistful of Darla's carefully folded football-shaped notes on his desk where they landed like dead butterflies. One by one, he unfolded them, read them, and locked in on me over his reading glasses, getting increasingly furious with sweat dotting his forehead, the first drops of rain before a storm.

"My God. Darla Harms wrote these?" I shook my head yes as he pushed his glasses up to study my answer. Like many men in the community, Mr. Moore probably knew Mr. Harms from hunting. Everyone knew of the Harms, if not for the never-ending supply of deer urine he sold, for jerky and pit beef sandwiches he fired up in the brick grill behind the store for his customers. "I'm going to have a little talk with Miss Harms and the other kids. If they say one more word to you, you let me know. This is going to stop right now," he said, wiping his forehead with a handkerchief. "You're staying on that bus."

Later that day, Darla sauntered up to me with eyes squinted and her mouth pouting like a curled up worm on a sidewalk. "I talked to Mr. Moore about your little problem…"

"You mean you," I said bluntly and kept walking, feeling the full power of taking control of a situation and ending it for good.

The terms of my grounding sentence allowed me to work out at the Y or baby sit. When I earned money, certain accounting measures had to be followed. When I came home from babysitting, my mother snatched the money still warm from the babysitting father's wallet, and stuffed it in a jar. If I wanted to spend any of the money I earned, I had to itemize what I planned to buy and obtain my mother's approval, a process that many parents could stand to emulate if they have shoplifting kids. The last thing I wanted to do was go through this process. Instead, I took every babysitting job that came my way just to get out of the house.

When I came home from babysitting one night, my mother sat in the middle of the sofa looking at me with a twisted, giddy smile on her face, as if she could barely contain her excitement from winning the lottery. Instead of stretching her hand out to collect my earnings, she pointed to a small cardboard box sitting on the coffee table in front of her.

"Look what I found," she said, sliding the box towards me. I reluctantly lifted the lid, and every single piece of heirloom jewelry that was supposedly stolen from our house glittered back at me. Just like that, all of her support, supposed love, and attempts to "help me through this" drained out of me. Without a word, I dropped the box on the table with a heavy thud, ending any hope of continuing a relationship, much less trusting her. When I found out she had hidden the box herself, I realized this entire party/rape drama was orchestrated by her, for her. Deep inside me, my hopes of having any kind of mother-daughter relationship curled up and died right there inside that tattered box. She had turned a corner from just acting like a bitch to cruel. A choice was made – and it was clear to me that the choices she made were always self-gratifying.

Identifying my mother's true motives: to destroy my spirit, crystallized everything in my mind. Every gesture she made from then on, nice or not, would be met with doubt and scrutiny. My world reorganized itself, and she returned to her rightful place as my enemy. At the same time, shutting the door on my mother's madness opened up opportunities for me to experience life as a typical junior high school ninth grader. But this time, with a brand new defense: happiness.

> *"Some people have take-out for dinner...*
> *My family had take-down."*

16 . KID WAR

The week before ninth grade, I dreamt I was sitting on the brick wall outside of Addison Junior High. Pink cherry blossoms fluttered around me like snow. Suddenly, I floated high above the trees. When I looked down, I saw myself with a boy sitting next to me. He leaned over and kissed me. I felt myself falling backwards, feeling the warm, dreamlike sensation of prepubescent love. A psychic once told me that if you saw yourself in a dream, it would come true. That's how I knew everything in ninth grade would be totally different than eighth grade.

Everything changed the minute I became friends with Jenny again and met Jane. Even though I "got weird" in eighth grade, not to mention named school slut, Jenny decided it was safe to be friends with me again. Although Jane Anderson vaguely knew of me during my brief stint as a "freak," she also became my friend. Jane gnawed on sour apple-flavored Now and Later candy and whipped through calculus problems like she was filling out her name on a form. Her hair shined the color of honey and always curled under perfectly in the back, no matter what. It took me thirty minutes with two brushes, a curling iron and blow dryer, and mine still flared out like a bird tail. Jane had a subversive sense of humor, while Jenny's was outwardly hilarious, punctuated with the comic timing of a professional.

When Matt announced the new "dirty" word he learned: "organism," Jenny said, "Is that what you have, Matt? Organisms?" When Jane studied each angle of a single Dorito before nibbling off a corner, Jenny popped, "What's it say, Jane?" Jenny had the charisma to present herself as someone much older, once talking it up with some Navy midshipmen and getting us invited to their Ocean City condo for kamikaze shots. Jenny's ability to charm her way into situations made her older sister insanely jealous. It was screaming fun watching her sister detonate when we'd get invited to parties with her sister's friends.

The two of them quickly took up for me when we became friends, calling Cece "Little Toke" Flynn a thief for stealing the contents of my room. As I walked out of biology one day, Joy "Big Toke" Flynn, Cece's big sister, slammed me face first into the lockers.

"You quit telling people my sister is a thief, or I'll beat your fucking face in," she yelled at me, her raspy voice reeking of cigarettes and pot. With all the commotion in the hall, none of the teachers noticed she had her clammy hand around my neck. "If you tell one more person, I'm going to fuck you up. You hear me?"

Here was eighteen-year-old Joy Flynn with her leather jacket and pot leaf necklaces, threatening me, Little Miss Eighth Grade Preppy Pants. I straightened my white oxford shirt, adjusted the pink polka-dot ribbon in my hair, and headed to the bus realizing Mr. Hagwood was right, I am nothing like them. And, the decision that I never wanted to be anything like them cemented itself in my mind and set me on a better course. The party drama ended right there. My life started approaching teenage normal.

Jenny, Jane, and I spent weekends staying up all night watching scary movies and *Prisoner Cell Block H*, a British drama about a women's prison, prompting me to spout off, "Prison cells are so not like that." Jane just looked at me, but Jenny knew all about my brief imprisonment after shoplifting. The closest we came to getting in trouble was hustling Tickle Pink Boonesfarm from York Road Liquor Depot, dumping it in Arby's cups, and sucking it down with a straw. The drinking age was still eighteen, so we easily got our junior school hands on alcohol whenever we wanted. On Saturdays, we rode horses on trails off of Providence Road. On weeknights, we constantly ate dinner at each other's houses, which provided a whole new perspective on the daily operations of families.

Going to dinner at Jane's was like stepping into a TV show. The Anderson's oval table sat dressed crisply with a linen tablecloth. Mr. Anderson took his place at the head of the table while Jane, her older brother, Al, and sister, Lily, sat down. Mrs. Anderson sported a dress with pearls and apron and actually talked nice to her kids. Just like a '50s TV mom, she politely announced: "Girls, time for dinner," a stark contrast to my mother's invitation to: "Get your asses in here."

When Mrs. Anderson sat a tall glass of frosty milk in front of me and I recoiled, I thought she would explode like my mother would have. Instead, she apologized profusely for not knowing I hated milk as if there were some way she could have known, just like Mrs. Cleaver would have done. When Jane asked my mother to kindly not put a tomato on her hamburger, my mother threw the tomato at her, sending Jane running down the hall and earning her the nickname: "Tomato Butt." Terrifying moments like that might have sent Jane running home for good, but instead, she thought it was funny and kept coming over for more. I once asked her if she could recall anything positive about my mother. "She kept a clean house," she responded blankly.

Sitting at the head of the table, Mr. Anderson commanded all the presence of head of household. Before the roast came in for a gentle landing in the middle of the table, Mr. Anderson looked at me and said, "So, you're an RC."

"Dad," Lily and Al both protested.

"Cola?" I said, completely lost, as Al busted out laughing.

"Roman Catholic," Jane said.

"Dad, stop it. Don't listen to him, Jacki." Lily's flawless porcelain skin flushed like an embarrassed baby doll. The Roman-Catholic exchange was the most controversy I personally witnessed as a guest at the Anderson dinner table. Their dinners seemed so civilized compared to ours. No one chased kids around the house or sent cusswords flying.

Dinner at Jenny's house was completely casual because as the only parent in the house, her mother worked like crazy. Jenny sobbed on my shoulder the day her father moved out. She seemed to be getting used to having an occasional dinner at her father's apartment. Her mother might have worked a lot, but she was never too busy to leave us nice notes on the fridge and money to go get ice cream at the 7-Eleven up the street. So Jenny learned how to make her own dinner, dousing chicken breasts with Italian dressing and roasting them to perfection in the oven. We pulled the coffee table up to our chins and stuffed down the seared chicken with a side of Doritos while watching the then-fledgling MTV.

As much as I loved going to Jenny and Jane's for dinner, they loved coming to my house even more. Our dinner table was shaped like a pool table. Everyone sat down as the bowls of steaming food broke and shot to all four corners. From one corner, my brother Bruce jumbled himself into his chair and kicked the table. Each glass tilted and produced quick spills all around.

"God damn it. Do you have to kick the table every night? So anyway Gary, I can't believe these homeless assholes, living out of a car. So I told 'em this is against the law. Move it, or I'll haul every one of your asses to the Ball County Detention Center."

Dad sat at the head of the table with his head slumped over. A slow whipping motion circulated fork to mouth, no matter what happened. He never said a word as Matt stood behind my mother making rabbit ears and stretchy faces behind her head. When she spotted his reflection in a picture on the wall, she wheeled her kid-whaling arm around, knocking an ashtray clear across the kitchen and chased Matt first around the table, then around the house. Dad concentrated on his lima beans as if he were dismantling a bomb. Tears poured out of Jane and Jenny's eyes as they laughed.

We kept eating as Matt did his Three Stooges, "wo-bo-bo-bo-bo" imitations in the background. Matt seemed to be having a good time until she caught him and applied her police chicken hold, making his arms and legs twist around like wire and his head gawk out literally like a chicken. Meanwhile, Jane and Jenny enjoyed the show, mouthing, "Oh my God," to each other. Just like any other night, Dad got up, cleared the table, and did all the dishes without saying a word. The next day at school, Jenny and Jane gave a full report before the bell rang, making me an instant junior high school celebrity.

"Man, I wanna eat dinner at your house, Eberstarker," George Atler said. "The most exciting thing at my house means having pizza with pineapple instead of pepperoni." Kevin Daily, George's quiet best friend, just laughed. Soon we all became the do-everything-together, best friends, except drink Boonesfarm. Kevin and George didn't drink; they played sports. I wondered what they thought of us sometimes since we drank and went to field parties. Kevin soon became my first real boyfriend. All the teachers gawked at us and said, "Ah, young love." "Barf," I'd say back, making them shake their heads. "You just wait, Jacki Eberstarker, you'll remember these moments the rest of your life," they'd call after me in the hall.

Ninth grade was just like my dream – a whole new life with the boy in the dream played by Kevin. We'd sit on the brick wall, and he kissed me as the cherry blossoms drifted to the ground. With hair and eyes the golden color of syrup, I called him "Fox." When he kissed me, his eyes welled up with tears. For once, I felt like I belonged. But all of my good-grade earning, good-behavior wielding, first-love-displaying giddiness disgusted my mother. Even my good behavior had to be stopped.

Having an official boyfriend gave her all kinds of new territory to harass me over and project her brand of sexuality on me. "You look like a slut, are you trying to make it easier for him to feel you up?" "No boys in the bedroom," she said, reminding me, Oh yeah, we can make out in my room. But I didn't let her get to me. Suddenly, my happiness became a power in itself, and she didn't know what to do with it.

With the connections my mother made through the society families I babysat, you would have thought ascending to a higher social level would have made her happy. Replacing the Bonneville with a new Volvo and ditching a wool coat for a full-length fur one effectively informed the Bridlepath neighbors: "We've got money now." Getting invited to some of what I still referred to as "phony parties" let all the neighbors know: "We not only belong, we were invited." And if my mother wasn't invited, she joined their pyramid schemes, hawking everything from vitamins to magical cleaning solutions and poster "art." But none of that was enough.

Although she was invited to the parties, she scrambled to do whatever it took to secure her next invitation, even scrubbing the floors after the guests left. I once overheard a group of ladies saying my mother's dress made her look like a ghost, then laughing at how they wish she'd come over and clean their houses.

A surge of sadness and embarrassment washed over me; I actually felt sorry for her. Then, I just got angry, remembering how we warned her that an ivory dress on anyone with powder-white skin would look scarier than a Scooby Doo apparition. She must have imagined herself as looking fabulous and refused to listen to anyone.

While my mother focused on my every move, she started hammering my brothers more and cut my father down loudly at parties, which inadvertently pulled us back together as a team with Dad as our captain. But this time, enlisting Jenny and Jane for back up escalated the situation to a full-blown war. With all of us growing older, the stakes were higher when my brothers started fighting back.

Matt operated covertly, slipping cigarette loads in every one of her cigarettes. As she lit each one, "Pow!" until the entire pack was destroyed and all the frayed cigarettes sat around the ashtray like singed scarecrows steaming in a hot tub. Bruce took advantage of his size and took her on physically, once locking himself in his room and calling her a bitch. "If you call me a bitch one more time, I'll kick this door down," she threatened.

"Bitch," he drew out extra long to get her extra special enraged. Three police officer kicks did the job, and the door panel popped out enough for her to wrangle her hand in and open the door. She attacked Bruce right on his bed, but he fought back, knocking her glasses off with a tennis shoe. When Dad got home, he was furious at her for damaging the door, not Bruce. Not getting back up from Dad no doubt made her feel hopeless. Meanwhile, Bruce retaliated using black magic and fashioned a voodoo doll of our mother made out of gray clay with hair he removed from her brush pressed into it.

"Take this, Bitchface," he said, stabbing the doll with a pin. With tight angry clay lips wrapped around a strip of paper rolled up like a tiny cigarette, the doll looked exactly like her, prompting Matt, Jenny, Jane, and I to fall on the bed laughing. Daily discussions focused on how to get rid of her, drawing equal bouts of disturbing laughter. We constantly talked about throwing her over a bridge so we could go out to dinner in peace, then realized she'd scale the side of the bridge, just to ruin our dinner. It seemed like that was always her motivation – to ruin something. Without realizing it, she was steadily destroying her own marriage along with any chance of having a relationship with her children.

Sensing a family implosion, Dad called one of his famous "family meetings." We all sat down around the kitchen table in our usual dinner spots. My mother seemed nervous, almost subdued, sitting on the edge of her chair and not smoking. Dad leaned forward and said, "We aren't getting along, and I don't know what to do about it. So I'm thinking about leaving."

Matt, Bruce, and I screamed "no" together. "You can't leave, Dad." Together, we sounded like one, big whiner in stereo, begging him not to leave.

"I'll run away," I said, jamming my feet down onto the orange and brown linoleum. "I'm almost eighteen. I'll leave." Dad glared at me.

"Yeah, us too," Matt and Bruce said, while my mother squirmed in her chair.

"Well, do you want me to leave?" she said, looking down at the table.

"Yes," Matt, Bruce, and I said in unison. But instead of getting up from the table and leaving, she just sat there and acted like she didn't hear us. That's when I realized she had no grasp on the way her actions affected others, like the time her co-workers put defamatory notes on her locker and she came home crying, conveniently forgetting about how she had called in sick on the same exact day every month. They were probably bitter because they were tired of covering for her. What a luxurious position it must be to never take responsibility for your actions. At the same time, what hell it must be waking up, wondering why no one is there for you.

"What about vacation this year?" she said, clapping her hands together as if that was what we were talking about the whole time. The subject of her leaving and granting us complete happiness was dropped right there. After a brief parental discussion, they struck a deal about summer vacation. Dad will take all the kids to Ocean City without her. Then, he would take her to Maine in the fall without us. But after she went through his wallet at a pool party and discovered "The List," the deal was off. For years, Dad had been recording everything she ever did to get on his nerves, with gems such as: "Blows nose and examines contents." To get him back, she showed up at our rented Ocean City beach house in his prized 1976 L-82 Corvette Stingray and promptly ruined what we had been calling our "Bitchface-free" vacation.

Despite the family drama, summer with Jenny, Jane, George, and Kevin was my best ever – going to Ocean City the same week, posing on the beach and getting kaleidoscope pictures taken, dousing Thrasher's Fries with vinegar at the boardwalk, and kicking through the sand from Maryland to Delaware beaches, then taking the bus back down Ocean Highway. Right before school started, my happiness dropped like a coin lost in a vending machine when I heard Kevin's friends making fun of "The Irene," a bubble-shaped hotel at the beach. Just like that, I knew. He had met a spirally-haired girl named Irene. He swore that "nothing happened," stomping my once buoyant puppy love heart flat. Just like that, our group ended.

Jenny, Kevin, George, and I started our first day at Redbrook High School while Jane went to Shellenwald High School. I sobbed through my freshman year, watching Kevin flirt with the Johnson Creek girls and share a locker with one of them – right next to mine. He never told me why he broke up with me, but I couldn't help but wonder if it was because I treated him the way my mother treated my father. Did I humiliate Kevin in front of his friends the way my mother embarrassed my father at parties? Or did he just want a prettier, more popular girlfriend? That question still haunts me. The teachers were right – I would remember the days of candy-coated first love forever and how it so easily disappeared.

> *"I told my boyfriend I felt suicidal...*
> *So he lent me his gun."*

17 . THE BOMB

During the week, the audience at the Comfort Inn Greenville, South Carolina, bustled with business people and travelers passing through on I-85. Mark Wyland, a professional comic, and I, drove there together when I got out of work one night. As I did my set, I could hear people saying, "That girl is really funny." Afterward, Mark told me about another female comic doing similar material who was "totally making it." Then, the manager awarded me a weekend slot at feature, a promotion for me. In comedy world, emcee was an entry-level position, feature meant middle management, and headliner designated top-level executive. Mark won the headliner spot. The pay for a feature act: Weekend accommodations at the Comfort Inn Greenville and $25 to work Friday and Saturday nights.

Suddenly, comedy had re-emerged as a gentleman suitor, and I got cocky. So I showed up for my weekend work thinking the audience loved me so much, I could wing my set with all-new, never-before-practiced material. But when I climbed up on the "stage," a plywood box with carpet stapled to it, the audience hated me right away. "Yeah, she sucks," a woman in the front said, as everyone in the audience laughed and joined in. "Get the little girl off the stage," a man jeered. All I could see from the stage was heavy work boots and flannel shirts, no suits. The traveling business people were gone. Not that a change of audience excused a bad set because I didn't actually have a set that night. The audience was mostly local men who came to mess with the comics, and I deserved it.

As an emergency measure, I jumped into my well-rehearsed bra set, but it was too late. So I experienced my first down-in-flames, full-set bomb. When Mark climbed on stage and reclaimed the audience's respect, the manager demoted me to emcee right then and there, a fate worse than death. My low-energy delivery did anything but excite the audience, so being an emcee was extra-special difficult for me. Plus, they hated me. Mark issued words of advice, saying, "What did you do that for? Always have your set ready. Always." After crying behind the juke box in the back of the club for a half hour, I got back on stage to close out the show, saying, "Oh yeah, and for that woman who said I suck, I do not. Just ask my boyfriend." To my surprise, the audience turned on the woman and issued my only applause for the night.

Later that night, a group of people who looked very similar to the rogue comics approached me at a diner, I thought, to beat me up. Instead, they said, "We thought you rocked. Greenville is like a Steven King novel – they don't get smart women. They couldn't understand your material if they tried. Don't take it personally." Bombing was supposed to be synonymous with learning and growing. I immediately learned to never come unprepared for a show, not to mention: Grow up, not everyone will love you – a fact that I was well aware of, but that the artificial high of applause had made me forget.

Returning to Atlanta all slumped over, more blows waited for me. After standing on a chair and doing a five-minute set to audition for open mic at Borders Bookstore, the manager invited all the other comics back except me. "She said you were 'Too Blue for Borders,'" my friend from comedy class, Sarah, explained. "She thought your training bra jokes were vulgar, what can I say?" I also took the Borders rejection personally, along with the fact that I had lost a comedy contest at a TV station. Convinced that my start at a comedy career was officially over now that I blew my chance to appear on television and was so bad, I couldn't even perform at Borders, I spiraled deep in depression. Trying to defy depression, I forced myself to keep going, standing on a window ledge and performing a set at a frozen yogurt store while all my comedy friends, even the rogue comics, went to Borders. My material was no match for the smoothie blenders.

Meanwhile, nightmares about a dark-haired little girl started haunting me. In the dream, the dark-haired little girl pulled me down grass hills into a dark, black well. The walls closed in on us, and her dress turned black with soot. So I lifted her onto my back and tried to climb out, but we tumbled back down the well. Night after night, the girl got increasingly angry at me, telling me she hated me. In subsequent dreams, she grew older. I tried to talk to her, but she turned away, saying, "I hate you." In the morning, I woke up as if I had never slept. My back throbbed, weight dropped off of me, and my face looked skeletal. I crawled back to the chiropractor, but still felt bad. I tried working out, then felt worse. Something was closing in on me, and I didn't know what to do. Intense pain filled me, and I got desperate to shake it off me. I wrote in my journal: "Everything in my life looks so different now that I've identified myself as an official loser. My life feels valueless. I feel invisible and dropped out of the world. Everything is falling apart – work, my relationship, comedy. I want my life back. I want to feel alive, but I don't. I need someone to protect me from myself."

When I got home from work that day, a letter from my father waited. Inside, a newspaper clipping read: "Priest's suicide opens issue of abuse." I panicked. Father Connor was our family priest at the rectory where my grandmother worked. She took me there sometimes while she worked, and I once got left behind in a confession booth for three hours thinking I surely was going to hell. Father Connor was the one who was too busy with the altar boys to pay me any attention. Although I have only positive memories of him at my communion, the news of his death crashed down on me. The next thing I knew, I was on the grass looking up at a tree as memories swirled violently around me like long spirals of leaves...

It's sixth grade at Colonial Elementary. I'm sitting at an octagon-shaped table. The new carpet smells like nail polish. I duck my head under the table to get my tablet from under my chair. A hand grabs into my dress and tears into my crotch. I scream as his fingers wriggle inside my panties. It's Derek O'Leary, the kid who told me if I didn't win a game of Horse, he would "grab my pussy." The teacher immediately calls a conference with my mother to discuss my "under-the-table discussions in between lessons." I'm the one who gets in trouble, cementing the thought in my head: Getting sexually abused was my fault.

It's late at night at the Grayson's. I am twelve. A thunderstorm echoes in the distance like crashing waves and I watch TV sitting next to Peter. Mrs. Grayson is asleep next to me in Mr. Grayson's recliner. Peter pulls me over to him, slides his hands in my shirt right in front of his mother. Then, he opens my zipper with one hand. I clamp my hand to my pants and he bats it away. I am watching TV. He slides his finger deep into me. I am watching TV. He turns his face to kiss me and scrapes his beard across my cheek. His beard feels like wire on my face. When his mother stirs, he tosses me across the sofa like a throw pillow.

It's Christmas at the Grayson's. I am thirteen. Peter takes me up to his room alone to "play video games." He puts me on the bed with him and slides his pants off. Then, he takes my hand and rubs it all over his penis. My hand is all pins and needles like it's asleep. His penis feels soft and limp. When my mother pounds on the door, "Is Jacki in there?" he shoves me under his bed and tells her I fell asleep. "Okay," she laughs and walks away. My head hits the metal frame on the bed, my shirt is blanketed in dust. I stare at his Docksiders worn sideways at the heels under the bed until Peter orders me to get out from under the bed and leave.

I am fourteen, tanning out in the backyard in my bathing suit. Peter calls me over. He says, "Come 'ere, I want to show you something," and acts like he's leaning over, but he pushes me into a corner of the porch instead, unties my bathing suit top, and puts his mouth on my breasts. I think to myself that they are about the size of a single dip of ice cream and fit right in his mouth. Then, he kisses me full on the mouth, running his tongue deep into my throat. Behind Peter, I see a neighbor duck back into a dark corner of his garage and feel like he will think I am a slut.

I am fifteen. Peter takes me to a festival with his friend, then pulls his Porsche into an open field so they can smoke pot. When his friend leaves to go to the bathroom, Peter leans me across his lap and kisses me long and hard, working his hand up into my shorts. When his friend returns, Peter shoves me between the seats. Later he jokes, "Hey Jacki, wanna take a walk in the forbidden forest?" right in front of his friend. Maybe he thought joking about it meant he didn't do anything wrong? Maybe he never realized girls grow up to be women who remember.

I'm in eighth grade. I am at McDonald's with Priscilla and Darla. We meet some guys at the state fair. Priscilla goes behind a dumpster to make out with one guy. Darla is on the sidewalk talking to some other guy. A boy comes up to me and asks me to go behind the building with him. I go because I want to be cool like Priscilla. My body tingles numb as he slides his hands in my jeans and moves his fingers up into me. I feel as filthy as the asphalt for letting him do it. When he asks me to give him a "blow job," I walk away because I have no idea what that means. Soon after, Priscilla and Darla pronounce me "school slut," a label that sticks.

I am nineteen and in college when I visit Mr. Hagwood before Christmas break. He asks me to give him a "Christmas kiss" before I leave. So I hug him, and give him a peck on the cheek. Then, he says, "You can do better than that," shoving me up against a stairwell and forcing his tongue down my throat. My knees shake violently as I walk back to my car. This realization saddened and disappointed me. Mr. Hagwood was my biggest proponent and probably saved my life in eighth grade. Did he help me with the intent of eventually hitting on me?

The memories washed out into darkness. I stared up at the trees stretching far up into the black sky. A whisk of a cloud brushed the front of the moon. I thought to myself, Take a good look. This is the last time you're going to see the sky. As I realized I could not live with myself or these truths, the sound of a cricket punctuated the air. Sadness closed in on me as I saw my life in a completely new light. The people I trusted let me down. The men I loved and thought were trying to protect me were actually predators. My whole life was a lie I realized I could no longer live. The shock of realizing that the men I thought loved me and were trying to protect me were actually predators filled me with searing pain. The secrets I did remember must have made an invisible "Welcome. Sexually Abuse Me Now." sign that invited predators all around. Getting blamed when boys at the community center groped me, a boy in sixth grade grabbed me under the table, or a man "raped" me in eighth grade reinforced my understanding that I had somehow invited their behavior. It was my fault. My affair with Paul was really about a pedophile and his victim, not two people tangled in love despite an inconceivable age difference. At the same time, I gained clarity about my behavior of numbly walking into sex with people. It seemed like I had to do whatever people wanted me to do. Instead of protecting myself, I simply left my body and got it over with.

Dark secrets had been pressed so flat in my mind, I never saw them. The secrets I did remember and the ones that were repressed merged, amplifying a painful truth: I was only what others needed me to be—an object meant solely for people to fondle, take advantage of, victimize, and control. All my life I've laughed at everything that has happened to me, but not now. Whatever fragile foundation I had as a person was completely gone. I stood at zero with no hope. Only one decision remained: How was I going to end my life?

"Eberstarker? What are you doing out here, man?" Trixie said, looking down at me with a plaid skirt on. "Oh my God, what's the matter?" She kneeled next to me and scooped me up in her arms. "It's that Aston bastard again, isn't it? What did he do to you?" I told her what happened, and Trixie took me inside and cried with me on my bed as I sobbed uncontrollably. Then, she reluctantly called Aston to come over. He listened patiently, for once, and held me as I cried. Then, he pressured me to have sex with him and got furious when I said no. The next day, Trixie pleaded with me before she left for work, "Please don't do anything crazy to yourself, Eberstarker. Remember all the people who love you, like me."

From that night on, all I could think about was ending the pain. The only way I saw to do that was suicide. The sensation of being afraid of what I would do to myself was so terrifying, I would have been safer being alone in a closet with Ted Bundy. It was as if my body wanted to kill itself to make the pain stop. Even when I meditated, my "happy place" turned into a cliff. I visualized jumping. Suddenly, I heard the voice of a man in my head. But instead of telling me to kill the neighbor's cat, the voice made sense. He said I didn't know him, but he was there to protect me. "Go back to your life, Jacki," the voice said, and was gone. I wasn't sure if the voice was a ghost, spiritual guide, or if I really was crazy. Later, my therapist told me people in deep depression sometimes hallucinate.

Visually, I jumped. As my body lofted in mid-air, a surge of regret hit because it was too late to turn back. Suddenly, it occurred to me that I might not be able to stop myself from doing it. When I took a shower, I found myself experimenting with different razors and calculating that the cheap disposable ones would take too long. Plus, I didn't want people saying, "A Daisy killed her." Since I was too depressed to shop for new ones, I thought about new approaches. Meanwhile, Trixie was onto me. "Don't do it, Eberstarker. I know what you're thinking. I know you're struggling, but people love you. People like me. Don't you dare leave me, or I'll kick your ass." I was still pulling a suit on and going to work as usual. So I was shocked that what I was going through was so transparent. People at work kept asking me what was wrong, saying I seemed so "distraught." I lied and told them I was fine.

Although I had the best friends on the planet, I was ashamed to ask them for support. On the outside, I kept up the appearance that I was depressed, but still functioning fine. I wanted to tell my dad, but didn't know how. So I told him I was in serious trouble. His response: "You're taking therapy too far." At that point, I thought I was genuinely crazy and that I had somehow made all of this up. His reaction made me feel like I was doing something wrong asking for help and that he thought I was crazy, too. Knowing I couldn't play the Eberstarker denial-based "don't think about it and it won't hurt you" game anymore, I isolated myself from my family. I felt thankful that Aston was back in my life and clung to him like a life buoy, but instead of helping me, he plunged my head under the water and held it there. He must have wanted the drama of having his girlfriend commit suicide, because he lent me his loaded gun under the pretense of self-defense. I kept it under my bed, but had no intention of using it. Just like I decided in eighth grade, it would have been as if my mother pulled the trigger herself. So I gave the gun back and worked on another plan.

Jumping, I decided, would work best. Trixie wouldn't have to deal with a mess, and maybe they'd never find me in the river. A sense of relief washed over me that I had made a decision how I was going to end my life. It would require a trip to a bed and breakfast I loved and a long hike to a bridge in North Carolina. But before I left, I decided to see my therapist one last time and told her, "Thank you for everything you've done for me. I feel like I have to kill myself."

"I looked hot in leg warmers... Now I've got PTDD... Post-traumatic dress disorder."

18 . LOIS LANE

Redbrook High School. Junior year. Third period. Miss Wilson's algebra class.

"Well, if you're gonna sit next to me, we might as well get to know each other. My name's Carolyn," the girl sitting next to me said, offering a handshake. Wispy bangs fanned across her forehead, her red hair was pulled back into a thick strawberry-hued mane, and her brown eyes were the size of salad plates.

"Hi, I'm Jacki," I said, terrified. Carolyn was fierce enough to crush anyone, but also compassionate enough to defend her friends. We became fast friends, sneaking into bars, going to parties, and staking out boys in her pea-green Pacer.

Every day, Miss Wilson walked around to inquire how the homework was and did you, indeed, partake in the assignment. "How was it for you, Carolyn?" she asked, leaning over our desks, with her red pen and grade book in hand.

"It was really scary at first, but I did it over and over, and it felt really good then," Carolyn said, massaging her pencil suggestively while Miss Wilson studied Carolyn's answers on her homework.

"Oh, good. Glad to hear it, Carolyn," Miss Wilson said, moving on to the next desk as my ears popped inside out from the pressure of trying not to laugh. In the midst of reviewing quadratic equations, Carolyn got called on, making me wince.

"So this one was more difficult for you, Carolyn?" Miss Wilson said.

"Well, I wouldn't put it up there with the Hindenburg or anything," Carolyn said a little too sharply. Miss Wilson looked blankly at her like a bird that just landed on a windowsill, pumped its head twice, then hopped to the next equation. Then, it hit me: What would happen if I added Carolyn as a variable to the Eberstarker family dinner equation? What would Officer Eberstarker do?

Let's find out, class.

A glass platter sat on the table filled with chicken breasts that had been individually wrapped tightly with twine to keep the ham and cheese of the chicken cordon bleu contained. Carolyn sat quietly next to me as my mother plopped one strung up chicken per plate.

"What's this?" Matt said, poking at the twine.

"Yeah, what are you trying to do, kill us?" Bruce said, as my mother slammed the serving spoon down on the table.

"Shut the hell up. It's twine. Cut it off, you idiots." Carolyn leaned back in her chair as if she were slowing down a horse. Dad quietly sawed at his twine from the head of the table. My mother launched her nightly bitch session about her police officer day before she sat down. Dad never talked about work at dinner. Actually, Dad never talked.

"So all these assholes are rubbernecking at the accident and tying up traffic. Can you believe that, Gary?" His tie gently folded as he leaned forward with each bite and untied his chicken, which slowly uncurled on his plate. Then, Carolyn cut in.

"People are naturally curious about an accident," she said. "Of course, they want to see what's going on." Forks froze in mid-air. My mother's head snapped around as she issued a "how dare you" glare at Carolyn, but the effect was lost on Carolyn who locked in on my mother. Ready to take her on.

"They," my mother stuttered. "They should mind their own business."

"I'm just saying it's only human nature," Carolyn continued as if she were delivering a Debate Club speech. "People want to make sure everything's okay, that's all."

"Well, then *I* have to clear traffic and *I* have to maintain control of the accident scene," my said, emphasizing the word "I" as if the entire police force was composed of only her.

"Oh Mom, you're such a cop," I delivered as flat as the pounded chicken breast, making Carolyn spurt out a stream of iced tea into her napkin.

"Shut up, you sass mouth," my mother hissed, making me smile.

Watching Carolyn unseat my mother was all the proof I needed to realize one powerful truth: It could be done. Even with weapons and martial arts training, I was amazed that my mother could be intimidated by a sixteen-year-old's wit. Unfortunately for her, I ran with it, making a sport out of challenging her. Sure, most teenagers did that without fear. But I took her on, knowing full well she wasn't above using her service revolver to silence me permanently.

"No heavy petting," she screamed at me about my first serious boyfriend, Andrew, prompting me to respond: "Actually, I was planning on heavy grooming with a wire brush first." We fought constantly. Instead of holing up in my room like I used to, I stayed in the ring. One night, my father stepped in and tried to forge a peace agreement.

"Why can't you two get along?" he said, bringing us both into the kitchen for a talk.

"Here's the deal," I said calmly, then turning to her. "You have been my enemy since the day I was born. You can beat me and scream at me all you want, it's not going to change how I feel about you."

"Make her stop, Gary," my mother said, genuinely hurt and starting to cry.

"There's nothing you can do to make me like you. You treat me like shit," I continued, feeling a huge sense of relief finally getting to say how I feel.

"Jacki," Dad said, more upset about the cussing than the missiles I launched at my mother.

"After all the nice things I've done for you. The birthday parties, the nice Christmas presents, the clothes..."

"The beating the shit out of me and calling me names. Yeah, right. Don't you realize you ruin anything nice you do?" I jumped off the counter and walked to my room as my mother sobbed, still completely unaware of her behavior. Later, Dad continued to push the issue, saying, "She's still your mother." Apparently, he was trying to hold onto that lame Catholic ideal that you have to love your parents no matter what they do to you. That never worked for me. Between having Carolyn as a best friend and Andrew as my not-easily-threatened tall lacrosse player boyfriend, the strength to stand up to her gained power on its own.

Andrew effortlessly made all A's and played defense varsity lacrosse. When I got cut for failing to execute full twists in the dance company audition, my face stuck to the vinyl letters on his lacrosse jersey as I bawled. He convinced me that my talent would spin past the Redbrook High dance company. He seemed so much wiser than even adults. He quietly devoured books and aced classes, while having the wisdom of someone much older. He was onto my mother's manipulation from the first time he met her, telling me, "This isn't normal. You don't have to like your parents when they act like that. She wants to ruin everything about you, you know that?" The confirmation that my family situation was not like everyone else's saddened me. My eyes felt like they were welling up with honey, dispensing slow, heavy tears. The aged ones that had been waiting to reach their prime before they fell. I buried my head into his chest as my mother flashed the age-old parental porch light, then screamed, "Get the hell in here, or you're grounded for life."

Soon I realized how right Andrew was when my mother made my father miss seeing us leave for Andrew's prom. Dad had the flash loaded with fresh batteries and extra canisters of film lined up on the kitchen counter. But when I came swishing downstairs with a purple taffeta prom dress on, they were gone.

"Oh, your father is going to be so upset. He was so looking forward to this," Mrs. G said, running across our lawn barefooted, as I struggled like a bride to avoid crying. "Don't cry honey, you'll mess up your mascara. Now give me that," she said, fumbling with the Nikon. "How in the hell do you work this thing?" Andrew was right. My mother convinced my father we were leaving later and lured him to go look at plants.

"It won't happen forever," Andrew said, squeezing my hand. "You'll get out of here, and she'll never be able to touch you." That's what I had always hoped for, starting a new life somewhere else where I could transcend everything bad that had happened.

The summer after Andrew and Carolyn graduated, I returned to Redbrook alone. "Boy are you going to be lost without all your class of '83 buddies," the vice principal said as I slumped down the hall feeling sorry for myself. Andrew told me to put myself on autopilot and just get through it. So that's what I did. Eventually, I made my way into a new group of friends. We weren't the "pretty people" cheerleader crowd, but we were still active in school functions. We won second place in the "Gong Show" for doing a goofy dance on our knees with sheets over our heads that my dad said was hilarious. Later in my senior year, I helped organize Sports Night, the egg-tossing, tug-of-rope-pulling battle between the classes.

The night of Sports Night, my mother and Mrs. G sipped tea in the kitchen. Since she was laughing with Mrs. G, I figured it would be a good time to ask to take the Oldsmobile Custom Cruiser to Sports Night. If Dad were home, he would have let me drive it just so he could call it "The Teenage Love Bus" really loud in front of my friends.

"Can I take the wagon to Sports Night?" I asked my mother. "I've got to pick up some banners, and Jeanne and Kelly need a ride." She took one, long, contemplative drag on her cigarette, then threw up the roadblock.

"No you can't either," she said, blowing a straight "Police Line Do Not Cross" trail of smoke in front of me.

"Why not?" I said, trying not to whine.

"Because you're gonna get in an accident, and those girls are going to get hurt. Then, their parents are going to sue us," she said, as if she were explaining something that had already happened.

"What?" I half-laughed, it sounded so ridiculous.

"I'm not taking that kind of liability. Let them drive you," she said, knowing there wouldn't be time for them to drive all the way out to my house. They lived near school.

"Oh, Pat. Let her go," Mrs. G tried to convince her with an "it's no big deal" tone because it really wasn't a big deal. I drove that mammoth wagon back and forth from school all the time, enjoying the V-8 engine and four-speaker cassette player.

"You're not driving and if you don't shut the hell up, you're not going at all." She took a defiant sip of tea, while her response cranked the burner under my patience on high.

"You're just showing off in front of Mrs. G," I said bluntly, hoping to set her off.

"That's it, smart ass. You're not going anywhere now." She dove her cigarette into the ashtray and crashed it.

"Fine," I said and called my new friends Jeanne and Kelly right from the kitchen phone so she would hear every word.

"Hi, Mrs. Bradley? Could you tell Jeanne I can't drive to Sports Night because my mother says I'll pop wheelies, cause a fiery explosion, maim your daughter, then you'll sue us? ...No, we didn't get a new car. It's still the Oldsmobile... No, I don't need a ride, my mother won't let me go tonight...I know I'm on the committee. Oh, you'll tell Kelly, too? Okay, thanks."

Feeling the air molecules about to explode, Mrs. G escaped out the back door. Meanwhile, I prepared for battle, hoping for the first punch in a nice fistfight. Instead, she slammed both hands down on the table and yelled, "That's it. You're grounded." Then, she stood up, I thought, to attack me. Instead she stomped around the counter, turned the range on, and started heating up a stockpot.

"Oh, good. Thanks," I said with mock relief. "My senior paper is due, and I've got to work on it anyway. Actually, it would be better if you grounded me next week too, that way it'll get done on time," I said, using a twisted, cheery voice. The few times my anger escalated to that level, my voice stayed eerily calm.

She started shaking as she stirred the pot, clearly not expecting such a fight out of me. "Just wait 'til I tell your father."

"What, that I'll get my senior paper in on time? Yeah, he'll be really relieved. That way, I can graduate and get the hell out of here." She threw the wooden spoon she was using at me, delighting me. Giving her the opposite reaction of what she expected felt like scoring a game-clenching point.

When Dad came home, bowls of steaming spaghetti noodles and sauce and complete table settings waited, but my mother's space sat empty. She had retreated to the bedroom and shut the door. My father, brothers, and I sat around the table and eyeballing the food suspiciously, but no one would touch it. A brief discussion of "what if it's poisoned" and "what if there's glass in it" ensued. Then, Dad got up and poured it all down the sink, just to be safe.

Later that night, as I was sitting on the living room sofa next to Dad, my mother padded down the stairs for a snack. On her way back up the stairs, she yelled, "She's got her fat ass on the sofa again, Gary."

"Wow, I work out and everything. I thought I was losing weight."

Dad dropped his head into his hands. "What am I going to do," he asked me.

"Get rid of her," the words jumped out of my mouth as if they were caught in a fire. "I mean, Dad, you're not getting any younger. Don't you think you deserve a better life? Seriously." Again, I felt myself aging, dispensing "advice" to my own father. I couldn't believe I was telling him to get a divorce. I remember feeling incredibly sorry for him because he stayed miserable in the marriage for us, heeding the threat that she would take us. But I couldn't believe when he acted on it. Finally.

He stood up and walked upstairs as quietly as if he were going to bed for the night. There was a knock on the bedroom door, a quick murmur, and he came right back down the stairs.

"She'll be gone tomorrow morning," he said and went right back to working on the checkbook. Feeling paralyzed, I sat in silence with my "fat ass" still on the sofa. After being married for nineteen years, he must have considered leaving multiple times. For some reason, the "fat ass" comment became the tipping point, but I don't know why.

That night, I shoved furniture against my door, certain she'd use one of her police-issued service revolvers to shoot my head off. I figured she had one gun for every one in the family. My eyes stayed raccoon-open the entire night, just waiting for the door to get kicked down. Later, I found out my brothers also moved furniture in front of their doors. The next morning, she was already gone before the clock radios went off. But we weren't convinced it was for good until the moving truck came the following week. In the meantime, the news rippled over to the Grayson's.

"I just don't understand it," Mrs. G said. "Your mother would come over here and talk about doing nice things for you kids. Once, she talked about getting you a jewelry box that you wanted. She was so worried about getting you the right one. She wanted you to be so happy when you opened it."

"What?" my voice squeaked like Peter Brady's when his voice changed. "Are we talking about the same person? My mother?" Mrs. G kept talking.

"Then, the next minute, we'd hear her just laying into you over nothing. We just didn't know what to say to you kids when you came over here with your stories. We were horrified," Mrs. G said. "I just can't understand how a mother could hate her own children. And you're such good kids. Nice kids." She shook her head as she sipped her tea. "If she did love you, she sure couldn't show it."

We thought that because the Graysons made a joke out of everything, our family situation was semi-normal. Now we knew the truth. When I told Andrew, he was visibly relieved. Because now, he could come over and see me in peace without any hysterical porch light flashing and screaming episodes in the driveway. Carolyn just said, "It's about damn time."

We thought with our mother gone, all of our problems would be solved. We would finally be happy, just like our days sneaking off to dinner without her. But as nasty as she acted, she provided an anvil of balance and boundaries to the family. Without her, suddenly everything was a free-for-all with no rules, no boundaries, no limits. Bruce took full advantage of doing whatever he pleased while my father said nothing. Matt shifted from the Gifted and Talented to Angered and Lost, while my father said nothing. Meanwhile, I grew increasingly bitter that suddenly my brothers did whatever they pleased and no one in the family was remotely concerned about seeking therapy to straighten this out, except me.

The way we all acted after she left should have been the first sign that things wouldn't magically get better after she left, only worse. The first thing my brothers said was, "Well, now you're the woman of the house. Start cleaning. Start cooking." The first thing I said was, "Start kissing my ass. What do I look like, Betty Crocker? Make your own damn dinner." The last thing I wanted to do was take her place. As a group, we found twisted ways to celebrate our victory.

Since my mother had moved out the furniture in the living and dining room, we invited friends for sock speed-skating contests on the hardwood floors. That weekend, we had a blow-out party, with everyone singing: "Ding dong the bitch is gone." We tried to erase all evidence that our mother had ever lived in the house, tossing anything with her favorite burnt orange colors on it and clearing out Christmas decorations in the basement. When Bruce and Matt discovered an oil painting our mother must have had commissioned of herself, we turned our attention to destroying it.

After finding a can of red paint, the boys painted target circles around her beehive hair and draped shoulders and tossed darts at it, but they bounced right off. So they got out a BB gun. That worked. Pelting her portrait felt like relieving tension at first, not to mention payback for all the screaming, ruining, and controlling. Dad laughed so hard watching us, he cried. We had crossed so far over the line, it was hard to tell if there ever was one. The laughter we shared wasn't over a joke, it was more like a twisted payback mixed with the jittery fear of a family on the brink of imploding.

Any elation that she was gone dissipated quickly as Dad's worries set in. With only his income, he was left to support us three kids, three upcoming college tuitions, and a giant mortgage. The marriage ended quietly, with no contesting or courtroom drama. Since Bruce and I were over fifteen, there were no custody issues. Matt was younger, but our mother didn't fight for visitation or custody. Instead, she left it all up to us.

We reluctantly agreed to have dinner at her new apartment. The dining room looked out of proportion like a dollhouse with too-big furniture jammed in the miniature spaces. Things seemed different when she acted excited to see us at first, but her first explosion over dinner made the visit feel just like old times. As usual, she prepared a dish only she wanted to eat. None of us liked the massive amounts of peppers she packed in the dish, so none of us ate much, setting off her tantrum about how we were all such spoiled brat, pain-in-the-asses. That Christmas, we arranged another heart-warming visit. In the car, she started talking about ski parkas, so I mistakenly asked, "What's a ski parka?" to which she replied, "You're such a fucking, smart-assed bitch." Some trap door to my sanity permanently closed, and I said: "This is the last Christmas you're ever going to see me." I felt bad refusing her Christmas gifts, but I couldn't take any more. Not even a gift from her, because the price was always higher than I could repay. From that night on, she stopped calling us, and we stopped calling her.

At my high school graduation, a beaming Dad put his arm around my shoulder and someone snapped a picture. My mother and grandmother were invited, but I didn't see them in the crowd. Later, my mother called the house as we were laughing at the misspelled icing on the top of my graduation cake: "Happy Congraduation!"

"Where were you?" I said, annoyed that I didn't see them. Dad would have invited Grandmom and my mother to dinner with us, but we weren't sure they were there.

"You were standing with your father," she pronounced father as if it were a filthy word. So they did see me, but it was somehow my fault that they chose not to approach us. Without a grain of compassion for how strange it would have been watching your daughter graduate from outside the family, I spouted off in anger over all the times she treated me like the other woman.

"Where else am I supposed to stand? He's paying for college. That's the least I can do." She hung up on me. Once my mother threw a fit at my great grandmother's funeral because Dad held my hand as the grandchildren placed roses on the casket. I guess this was no different. Somehow his lack of attention to her was, once again, my fault.

When it came time to leave for college, Dad was more excited than I was. With my brain-dead S.A.T. scores, I was positive I wasn't smart enough to get into any college. That's why I took the first school that accepted me, Bridgewater College. But I was terrified I wasn't smart enough to be there and would fail out, which was what my mother repeatedly insisted would happen to me. My grandmother told me that my mother actually failed out of college. So I guess she wanted me to fail out, too.

Andrew commuted there and a couple of friends from my class lived on campus. So that made me feel a little better about going there. But the minute I moved in, I knew I was in trouble when my roommate informed me: "You owe it to yourself to try cocaine." I decided I had to get out of there before I went to my first class. With only 1,500 students, the culture stifled me. I was much more comfortable insulating myself with a sea of thousands of students. At Bridgewater, everyone knew everything about everyone. Meanwhile, Andrew and I were turning into different people.

I wanted to go to parties and meet people, he didn't. I wanted to go to Europe, he didn't want to leave his neighborhood. I wanted to leave Baltimore one day, he didn't. It didn't make sense. We loved each other deeply, but didn't like each other anymore. We broke up, got back together, and broke up for good after he spotted me dancing with another guy while we were supposed to be seeing other people. Years of bad relationship choices would follow, but I always thought that since a quality guy like Andrew could love me, I could find someone like that again one day. It just had to be statistically possible.

After one semester, I left Bridgewater for York University closer to home. The financial burden lifted off my dad, since York was significantly more affordable. But I found myself floundering in uncharted water, alone again. Andrew moved on and started dating someone else. Carolyn started modeling and had no time for non-models like me. I was treading water, desperate for a strong buoy of a friend to cling onto when suddenly a boat whisked me out of the water. At the helm: Leigh's teacher, Mr. Dorchester.

Jacki Kane

> *"We were soulmates in another life...*
> *Just not this one."*

19 . THE GLASS HEART

The City of Baltimore held immense opportunities for cheap college labor like me, which proved to be one undeniable asset of attending York University. Just as I went searching for the perfect public relations internship, an article surfaced in *The Baltimore Sun* about an historic maritime preservation center being built for underprivileged children – the brainchild of none other than Paul Dorchester. When I called him, he remembered me immediately.

"Bad Jacki," he said triumphantly.

"Bad Jacki?" I said.

"That's what Leigh called you, Bad Jacki."

"But I'm not bad," I said, surprised to hear that she called me that to Mr. Dorchester and even more amazed that he remembered me at all. He barely noticed me when I hung out with Leigh and him. Or so I thought.

"We'll see about that," he said.

For our first meeting, he picked me up in the same Audi he had when I was twelve and took me to McDonald's for breakfast. Being on the verge of entering actual womanhood made me feel as jittery as Bambi on ice. I wanted Paul to know I was not the dull public school duckling he probably thought I was when I was friends with Leigh. But I had no idea how to make him see that. So I wore a suit to the meeting, thinking that would make me as intriguing as a Danielle Steel character. Then, I tried to look alluring while peeling back the foil of my McOrange juice, sending a quick splash of juice all over my hands. He handed me a stack of napkins as questions about Leigh swarmed through my head. Did he still keep in touch with Leigh? Did she ever talk about me? Did he know why she dropped out of our friendship so suddenly? Did he know if we were ever really friends at all?

"So, do you ever hear from Leigh?" I bravely asked, then leaned away from the table as if the truth of his answer would jump out and bite me.

"Not lately. She came back to visit my classroom once, but it was a long time ago. I think she moved back to California," he said, stopping abruptly to crumple the foil from my orange juice.

I expected him to shift into talking business, but he cut straight to the boyfriend topic. Instead of delivering my usual "yeah right" self-deprecating cut-down, I tried for more intrigue.

"Nobody can keep up with me," I said. It was true, working at Netcom and going to school full-time made me relatively unavailable. But the biggest problem was that I wasn't attractive to college guys my age. Plus, with their focus on beer and multiple hook-ups, they didn't appeal to me either.

"I believe that," he said as his blue eyes expanded. He reached toward me and picked up his Diet Coke.

We talked business as I continuously brushed the sand of an Egg McMuffin off my hands, but it just kept pouring out of the wrapper like the sand in an hourglass, causing me to eat faster as if the sandwich would expire somehow. The Maritime Preservation Project was the perfect internship for me, since I could build it right into my college curriculum and earn credit. On a subconscious level, maybe I thought Paul could help me unravel the mystery of Leigh. Two birds with one stone I would have to dig through a quarry to find.

We talked more personal, although he refused to talk about himself. Now I realize he didn't want to acknowledge that he was married. He learned all about my job at Netcom and how I didn't fit in at school.

"You're Jacki. I can't believe you're Bad Jacki," he kept saying. I could feel his eyes fleeting all over me before glazing over and going somewhere else. Was he undressing me, I wondered, then slapped the thought from my mind. It couldn't possibly be true. I was eighteen. He was older than my father.

"You're Mr. Dorchester," I mocked him.

"Call me Paul, please," he said, as if calling him Mr. Dorchester caused him physical pain.

"Ready to go?"

When we pulled into the driveway, I noticed my dad had left for work and felt a sense of relief. Paul threw the Audi into park and leaned toward me, cobalt eyes blazing, "I don't know how it's going to happen or when, but somehow we are going to be together."

Heat rose up inside of me. What I said next felt like someone had taken over my body.

"I know," I said, feeling uncontrollable anticipation and complete dread mix like toxins.

Paul went out of state to run a summer camp, leaving me squirming for several weeks. I knew he would call me with an offer to be with him. I knew I would be faced with a yes-no decision, but had no idea what to do. Somehow, I knew I'd be powerless against yes. Suddenly, I stopped sleeping. Completely. Weight started shedding off me again. If I had understood the accuracy of instinct and listening to your body at the time, I could have steered clear of making such a dangerous choice. But I ignored all the warnings and knew I could not stop myself, or him.

No matter how wrong or unwanted, I yielded to male attention, thinking I'd better or take what I could get because there would be no one else. At the time, the only male I really wanted was my wound-tight lacrosse Netcom player boss, who constantly taunted me, but was engaged. A psychic told me he drove me crazy because I was like a squirrel and he was the nut that was just out of reach. She also informed me he only wanted me for sex. That was it. Because I so easily confused sex for love, I steered clear of that one. But this was different. A web of complex issues were woven into the relationship with Paul that I couldn't have understood at the time, and still don't. All I knew was that although my mind started to think, No. I heard myself say, Yes.

To relieve the pressure of the decision bearing down on me, I again consulted a psychic named Jane. When I sat down across the table from the psychic, the first thing she said was, "I see you're about to get involved with a much older man. Don't do it, honey. He will still help you with your career if you don't go through with it." I was amazed that she knew about Paul when I didn't ask any questions or tell her anything about me. "Besides, what would your mama say?" Her eyes, which were thickly rimmed with black eyeliner, bugged out as she said "your mama" and tapped her ruby nails across the tarot cards.

Right then and there, she instantly discredited herself. You'd think she would have known that I didn't give a crap about my mother, much less what she thought. Instead of dissuading me, her misfire about my mother fueled me with defiance. Now my hesitation about Paul had gelled into a decision: I was going through with it no matter what.

My full-time schedule at Netcom continued through the end of summer. I nailed my quotas and had already been awarded for sales and service performance. One day, I answered call number 119 out of the required 200 when the call came.

"Netcom Customer Service. This is Jacki. How can I help you?"

"Jacki." I froze. It was Paul drawing my name out as if it had four syllables. "I can't stop thinking about you."

"Same here." I prayed to the god of customer service that they were not monitoring this particular call. But then again, after the way my boss constantly teased me, I could see the benefit of revenge.

"I'm coming home early. Just to see you. I'm driving down right now, actually. Come over tonight. When I get back," he whispered, all throaty, as if he were half asleep. Instead, he was leaning into a phone booth on an interstate. I told myself that he was so enthralled with me, he drove back early. With that kind of attention, how could I possibly turn him down?

"Okay." Again, I couldn't believe what I was saying, and he picked up on it.

"You don't have to. You really don't. Are you okay with this? We can just talk," he said.

"Yes, I'm fine with it." My body went numb. I got so nauseated, I skipped the frozen microwave patty I brought for lunch and concentrated on taking more calls.

The woods filled in as black as ink as I wound through country roads to Jones Falls Expressway toward Paul's house. He lived in a rowhouse where any one of his neighbors could have easily seen me, but I imagined myself as invisible as I walked right through his front door and hoped the darkness would cover me.

We sat on the sofa, and he looked right through me. Then, he told me about his strained and sometimes violent relationship with his wife. He was in despair about what to do about her. She threatened to take him for everything he had, just like my mother did to my father. I fell directly into the trap of feeling sorry for him that he was in such a bad marriage and wanted to help him.

He soothed my nerves with the story of a sea captain's affair with a young maiden on the shore and how they kept it a secret for decades. He talked about lifting up out of this existence and into a realm with a different set of rules. I hung on every word and believed it when he said that we were not of this world. That we had been together in another life. With the kind of intense power he had over me, I still don't doubt that one.

He convinced me no one would understand our relationship and that was why we needed to stay outside of convention to be together. A decision forged in my mind. I decided to go through with it because a hunger was overcoming me. I didn't understand it, but knew I was powerless to stop it. I knew it was as wrong as shoplifting, but another side of myself had taken over. Again, I allowed him to gently pull me to the decision.

"You are so beautiful, and you don't even know it." His words intoxicated me and made my body limp. "You are going to be so amazingly successful, you know that? You have it all, beauty and brilliance. You mark my words– men will give up everything to be with you." No one has ever said anything to me like that before, probably because I was just a fledgling eighteen-year-old college girl. I gulped down the words as desperately as someone who was stranded in the desert who has just been handed water. He smoothed back the long strands of my asymmetrical '80s hair cut. "Don't you want to make it even with the short side?" he asked, smiling at me and getting closer.

"No," I laughed. "That's not cool." A jolt of embarrassment hit me when I realized I should have picked a more sophisticated word because now my age was showing. When he wove his fingers through my hair, I could no longer breathe. He pulled me toward him and kissed me slowly. I was amazed at my reaction as my body melted into his. I craved his attention like a drug. He turned off the light. The skeletal fingers of a tree scraped the window as he kissed me, and I wondered if anyone could see us. I felt like everyone did.

"I give great back rubs and front rubs," he said, sending a surge of panic through my body when I realized Leigh really wasn't lying when she told me those stories about "back rubs" and "front rubs" on Breighton School camping trips. I shut the thought from my mind as he led me into his bedroom and unbuttoned my shirt. I floated out of my body as his hands pressed into my muscles. He turned me over, ran his hands all over the front of me and followed his hands with his mouth. I wanted him to take me, but thought, God not here. On some level, I knew he wouldn't do that until he had tied down all of me like securing his boat before a storm.

It was four o'clock in the morning when I zipped back up the highway to go home. To keep from falling asleep, I rolled all my windows down and let the wind whip me in the face as Tina Turner belted out, "We don't need another hero" on the radio. I was falling fast and knew I was in deep trouble, but felt like someone had pushed me off the high dive, sending me straight toward disaster.

The lies to my family came easily after I split my life cleanly in two between college coed Jacki and Bad Jacki. Using my late-night college lifestyle easily covered up for my 4 a.m. return while working with Paul on the Maritime Project gave me plenty of excuses to spend time with him. We worked diligently on fundraising and arranged secret and not-so-secret meetings around our work.

One afternoon, he took me to a meeting with an international shipping mogul named Mr. Reese. His secretary led us into Mr. Reese's penthouse office, the inside of a diamond with faceted windows that revealed a full view of the Inner Harbor. The water traffic below looked like toy tugboats and sailboats drawing white lines in the bay. Mr. Reese, a suntanned, grey-haired man in a navy blue, nautical-looking suit, exemplified the word "debonair." As Paul started the meeting, I pushed my back up straight against the chair, took mental notes of every word, and stayed quiet. Toward the end of the meeting, Mr. Reese suddenly turned toward me.

"You're quite an impressive young lady," he said from behind his mahogany slab of a desk. "I wish I had that kind of composure when I was your age."

"She's going to be a huge success," Paul said. Suddenly, he beamed as if I were his daughter. Paul's pride filled up some empty pothole in my self-confidence.

"I can tell," the man answered. I was so caught off-guard, I overcorrected my posture and bounced my back off the chair.

After the meeting, Paul took me out on his sailboat. We carved through the spectacular day and swam as a few blue crabs sculled their way to the surface. At the end of the day, we anchored in a cove. I ran my fingers through his hair and pressed myself up against him. I could hardly stand it. I completely undressed him. He made love to me while darkness enveloped the boat. I felt an overwhelming sense of belonging. The only other time I felt this way was when Andrew and I finally got past the technicalities of how to have sex and allowed straight love and passion to make it happen the first time for both of us. Now I felt like I had a home with this man, and I wanted to cry. Someone loved me again, and I couldn't get enough.

We swam in the moonlight. I slid down the anchor line, wrapped my legs around Paul, feeling like one with him. He took me right on the bow of his boat as the moon watched. We drifted into a deep sleep as the lanyards pinged the mast like wind chimes. My heart turned to glass. When I was with him, it filled up rich red. By the end of our times together, the blood drained out of me, leaving my glass heart empty again. Each time I was with him, my glass heart would grow, leaving me increasing desperate to fill it.

To keep from thinking about him, I immersed myself at Netcom and played competitive volleyball at night. But it was more like monkey ball. I was the only player with any training, and it must have showed. One night, the official climbed down from the stand and called me over.

"You've played before. You really know what you're doing. I'd like you to try out for my junior Olympic team," he said as he flipped open his wallet filled with pictures of his kids. "Here, let me take your phone number." He wrote my number down on a business card and stuffed it back into his wallet. One thing I never realized about myself, and still don't, was that I actually was attractive. Attention from men was something that always caught me off guard, as if they were talking about someone else. My naivety combined with the pure desperation of having weak self-confidence must have become a beacon to predators. Soon, the volleyball coach started inviting me to weekend "volleyball retreats."

"Overnight?" I said, confused.

"Yeah, it's a blast. We all get cabins," he said as if we were dating.

"No, I have to work," I said, letting the irritated tone of my voice punch through the words.

"You're not going to make the team if you don't come," he said, getting increasingly angry.

"Sorry, I guess I won't be on the team then." I hung up.

His calls intensified. When he told me he knew where I worked and started threatening to find me there, Paul got furious.

"That sonofabitch. He's trying to ask you out. I'll take care of this right now," Paul ranted. His anger felt warm. I loved how it felt to be stood up for, except Paul did nothing to help me. I tried to tell my father, but he just looked blankly at me, then stood up and cleared the table. My boss at Netcom believed me and walked me to my car when I worked at night. Then, my anger and frustration gave me enough resolve to confront the situation head-on, starting with the head of the recreation council.

"You're making this up," he said arrogantly. So I called the Baltimore Police Department, who informed me he would actually have to assault me for them to take action. Meanwhile, the coach filtered his way through the Netcom customer service line and started harassing me at work. This time, I called his wife.

"I think you should know that your husband has invited me to go on overnight trips with him," I said, plain as day.

"Oh." She sounded still, but not surprised.

"The next time he calls me, I'm going back to the police." Suddenly, the calls stopped.

Fall swept summer away, and I moved into the dorms at York University. Paul snuck into my room and sat on my twin bed just looking out the window with me. When my suite mate banged the shared bathroom door, he popped straight up. I wondered if my roommate and suitemates knew what was going on with me and how lost I was. I wondered if they wondered about me.

That night, Paul and I went to get pizza, then ended up in the back of his

Audi. As he made love to me in a university parking lot, I left my body and stared blankly out at the dappled moon as my glass heart drained. Empty again.

We worked wonderfully together. As soon as my classes were out, I stayed on the phone for hours organizing fundraisers. I sat in audiences, trying to look innocent and indifferent while hanging on his every word as he spoke. As his intern, I dutifully carried out every task, writing press releases and raising money. But money seemed to evaporate at every turn, stressing Paul out. "I can only truly get peace when I'm with you, you know," he said, making me sad realizing how one-sided the relationship was. It brought me anything but peace. I started to feel a responsibility like I was literally saving his life by being with him. "I love you more than anyone will probably ever love you." He stopped himself. "That's probably unfair of me to say." Even now, I wonder if he ever really loved me at all. Instead, I suspect he loved that he was youthful enough to attract a college girl's attention.

In the dead of winter, finding places to meet in private became increasingly more difficult. Paul borrowed his brother's houseboat, and we met at the frozen dock. The ice-laced wind whipped at my legs, physically separating my nylons from the skin. We boarded the boat, calmed our nerves with vodka and Sprites like we usually did, and ate cheese crackers we picked up at the marina's vending machine.

"I love you, and miss you so incredibly much," I said, starting to cry.

"Little ol' me?" he said, flipping my mood from sad to furious. I hated when he said that.

"No, I was talking about someone else," I said, rolling my eyes.

"I just hope that one day, you don't regret that you've done this and hate me. I hope you realize that I will always love you."

"I make my own decisions," I said, lying to myself out loud. I did anything but take responsibility for my actions. He took my hand and led me to the bow, leaving our clothes littered all over the cabin in our wake. Just as he climbed into the bow with me, someone jumped down onto the boat. My heart filled with fire. It was his brother. Paul told me to stay in the bow. Then, he somehow got his clothes on and went outside to talk to his brother.

"It's okay. It's okay. It was just my brother. He thinks I was just napping in the bow," he said.

"Right. Napping with a pleated skirt on the floor? He knows now, doesn't he?" I said as I twisted a blanket tight around me like a tourniquet to squeeze my emotions tight and block them from gushing out in a torrent.

"He doesn't know who I'm with. But I'm telling you, he doesn't think anyone's in here." I believed him. He mixed me another drink and held me as my heart raced. When the sun dipped down into darkness, he said the dreaded words.

"I have to go," he said, giddily.

"How can you be so happy?" The blood drained out of my glass heart like a sieve.

"Because I can live on these memories alone."

"I can't," I said, devastated again.

"Who's to say we don't end up together? It would be crazy, but who's to say?" he said. The thought of marriage had never occurred to me.

Christmas was the loneliest I had ever felt. The month of December, we hardly saw each other. On Christmas Eve, we met for ten minutes behind Netcom, and he gave me gold earrings – fragile wisps of gold twisted into the shape of sailboats. As I gave him a wool blanket my father and I bought for his boat, I forced a smile on my face to hide my true feelings of disappointment.

"Wow, this is a really nice gift," he said, surprised. A sick pang thumped my stomach as I thought about how my father must have perceived my relationship with Paul. He would be so ashamed of me, but nowhere near as ashamed as I was, and still am, of myself.

My glass heart drained bone dry as I said good-bye to Paul. During Christmas, he went to the beach with his wife. Meanwhile, I hovered in between two worlds – my time with him and college life. It was desperately lonely not being grounded in either one. While Paul was gone, I stayed at home, sitting alone and staring out my window until my tears made the trees blur.

His image consumed me along with some feeling of obsession I couldn't explain. No matter what I looked at, the image of Paul sitting there staring into the swirling surf stayed in front of me. His eyes were clear blue frozen discs, and he had a slight smile. He was making love to me in his mind. I heard him laugh, "Jacki...Bad Jacki" like he was sitting right next to me. I was paralyzed, just sitting there on my bed with these images playing out like a movie. I sank lower into depression, sleeping for what seemed like days. When he returned, he immediately asked me to tell him which night he was thinking about me.

"Friday. Seven o'clock," I reported.

"You're right. That's incredible." He threw his head back and put his hands on my shoulders, but I didn't know whether or not to believe him or not.

"I could see you. I could feel you. I could even smell you. But I can't stand not being with you," I pleaded, just hoping he felt the same way, but he said nothing.

Later that winter, he took me to where his boat was dry docked in the middle of the night. It was so frigid, we never ventured out from underneath the pile of blankets. I wanted to hide under these blankets for the rest of my life with Paul. I wanted him to feel the same way. That was the last time I felt like I really meant something to him and his love was genuine. My glass heart glowed red once more.

When summer returned, the Maritime Project was ready to be opened with a grand, citywide celebration. I coordinated the ribbon cutting and handled another fundraiser. The day of the grand opening, the entire city stood still waiting for the hull to be lifted into the water. Helicopters hovered in the air; reporters stood stationed on the ground. People crowded on top of buildings to watch. Tugboats spouted water high into the air like liquid flowers. The mayor spoke, then Paul stepped up to the podium. Paul personally thanked everyone else in his speech, except me. After spending two years working on the project, my glass heart shattered as every ounce of self respect dropped out of me.

A philanthropist's daughter smashed a bottle of champagne across the bow of the boat, and the hull was lifted out of the shipyard, raised over the walkway, and lowered gently into the water with barely a ripple, setting off a great fanfare of boat and car horns sounding and wild applause. In the shipyard, a reception kicked off in the shipyard with a band playing, waiters bustling around, and people posing for pictures. I stood outside the chain-link fence, stunned. No one mentioned this event to me, and I clearly wasn't invited. Soon, my friends noticed me trying to hold back tears. One of my friends nudged me, "You should just walk right in there. You have every right to be there." But I knew I couldn't do that. Despite my work on the project, I realized Paul had kept me as invisible as glass to other people. Now I knew my place. Stress reducer. Sex object. Ego booster. Pacifier.

Suntanned and looking almost collegiate in a preppy khaki suit, Paul grinned for the photographers. His wife stood by his side, looking completely unimpressed by the whole scene. When Paul finally called a day later, I told him we needed to talk. Now.

We met at the marina. I pounded across the dock in my white tuxedo shirt and black skirt from working at my summer waitress job downtown. Then I climbed into the stern of his boat without getting near him. We sat out across from each other in the stern and talked as he fidgeted with the boat's silver wheel.

"Paul, I just can't do this anymore," I said.

"I knew this day would come." His head dropped. "Why?"

"I did so much work, and I wasn't even invited to the party. How do you think that makes me feel? Is that all I am to you? Just sex and a hard worker?" He pulled my head toward his chest as I started crying, kissed me on the mouth out in the open, and tried to blot my crying. I pulled away. "Don't."

"You're just so cute when you're mad." My anger shot straight up and dinged the bell like the game at the fair. With such raw hurt, how could he laugh at me? It was the first time I felt like the child I still was.

"How can this be funny to you?" I shot back. He straightened up.

"Whenever you have an event like this, it's inevitable that someone gets overlooked," he said in his official "talk to the press" voice.

"But it was me, Paul. Not 'someone.'" I couldn't believe what I was hearing. "How do you think it made me feel to not even get recognized? This is over." I could tell he had already drifted away from any feeling he ever had about me. Then, I wondered if he ever really had a genuine feeling at all.

"I said your name in my speech, but I choked up," he said. I didn't believe him. Then, he took a defiant tone. "If I have anything in my life, it's the memories of what we had." I couldn't believe he was already using past tense. "No one will ever, ever love you as much as I do," he said angrily while clamping his hands around my wrists. I used a defense move I learned as a lifeguard and twisted my hands out of his. Then, I climbed off the boat and left.

That day, someone was watching. Later, Paul told me he had received a call from a friend's daughter who saw us and thought I should know.

"So, Paul. I was at the marina today and saw you in a very compromising position. Who's the young girl?" she said. I'm not sure how he eeked his way out of that one, but as far as I knew, he did. Lucky for me, no one found out that I know of. Thinking about it now, I feel lucky I didn't end up at the bottom of the Chesapeake. What one of my scores of therapists told me: "He's a pedophile. You were clearly preyed upon." My therapists also tried to convince me to ease off holding myself so responsible for the affair, insisting he was a pedophile. Still, I just didn't want to believe that. But it made me realize how not special I really was and left me wondering, how many others were there? Was Leigh one of them? After hearing the expression "emotional vampire," I wonder if that's what I was? How did I become that way? I'd spend years learning how not to depend on someone else for self-worth and sustenance.

Soon after, he navigated his way through a fierce divorce. I talked to him on the phone, once, to ask him to provide a reference. He provided such an amazing reference, I landed a nice job at a Fortune 500 company. After that last contact, I only saw Paul in vivid dreams.

One night, I dreamt I was on a boat when Paul sailed up to me in another boat. My father sat next to Paul. But when I climbed aboard to see my dad, Paul disappeared. So was this whole thing with Paul a twisted way for me to plug in the holes of support I didn't get from others like my dad, or myself? Was I trying to reconnect with Leigh somehow or get closure on that? Maybe I'll never know. In the dream, I felt scared Paul would reach out, grab hold of me again, but not let go this time, pulling me straight to the bottom of the sea. Then the dream shifted, and I was at the harbor, searching for a storage closet I never found.

> *"I saw a ghost.
> She told me to get a life."*

20 . METAL DOOR

Trying to move on with my life was like jamming a puzzle piece in the wrong space and making the entire picture buckle. Since I didn't fit cleanly into the "College Co-ed" Jacki part of my life and wanted to run away from "Bad Jacki" as fast as I could, I found myself adrift again. Deciding to go with the parental advice I received in eighth grade turned out to be the best thing I could have done: Act my age and be a college student. So I completely immersed myself living the typical college experience – drinking all night, sleeping all day, gaining weight then getting blown off by eight guys, dropping weight then getting asked out by eight guys, etc. They even let me in a sorority. To the outside world, I looked like just another college girl. On the inside, hairline fractures spread across my sanity like subtle cracks in bone china.

Having time to react, not think, helped me avoid whatever was eroding my mental state, until family collided with college. My first year at Mountain State, which was actually my junior year in credits, Bruce had also decided to go there. My second year there, Matt enrolled. The campus was so huge, I thought I'd never see them, until they suddenly both got jobs serving dinner at my sorority house. Every night overwhelmed me as my brothers punched each other, saying, "Dick" while one walked out the kitchen's swinging doors. "Ass," the other shot back. Just like home, the one place I didn't want replicated. An irritation as familiar as the time my brothers followed Leigh and me into the woods and saw us smoking drove me crazy. I wanted my own life, not a dramatic re-creation of my home life.

To avoid my brothers, I had my meals wrapped up and ate by myself, but I still couldn't escape them. They attended every sorority social, dance, and party. Every day, they parked themselves in the TV room, watching *The Price Is Right* in between classes. At the time, I was too put off to realize they were probably just trying to hold onto what little thread of family we still had. Dad started dating a woman seriously who had a young daughter. So on some level, my brothers and I all must have known he would eventually move on to a new life that might not have involved us. I feared his new daughter, who would most definitely be smarter and nicer than me, would replace me completely. My mother turned out to be the pressure that held everyone together. With her gone, family as we knew it started eroding. I grappled at the edge of the family, fearful that I'd fall away like a chunk of earth into water below.

Meanwhile, my grandmother started calling me at all hours, drunk one day, sober the next. My image of her as the sweet grandmother I dearly loved and trusted, also started crumbling as she turned on me. "After all, your mother was a damn good mother," she snapped. "She worked damn hard. Damn hard for you kids. Who do you think you are? You should worship your mother. Yes you should." The next day, she called with a more muted, sobering speech, "Your mother was rough on you kids, this is true. And it's her fault you don't talk to her. I never agreed with the way she treated you kids. No, sir. You were good kids. Good kids."

Having the perception of my grandmother abruptly shift from fairytale memories of a mother-daughter-like relationship to suddenly unpredictable one with sharp edges and tangled webs forced me to grow up and see her clearly. It was as if she had died and was replaced by an evil sister. In another scotch and soda moment, she got into some crazy conversation about "dope," telling me "her Matt" would never do dope. Already late for class and jealous that she had suddenly started favoring Matt over me, I started losing my patience and made the fatal mistake of saying that her little, innocent Matt did indeed partake in his share of drug experimentation. If only I had known to keep my pie hole shut when it came to other people's business, especially my little brother's.

"Your Matt does drink. Your Matt does get high, so what?" The words flew out of my mouth like birds escaping a cage at K-Mart.

"Oh no he doesn't," she said with the same insistence she used arguing that JFK was the best president in history who never cheated on his wife. "My Matt does not do dope. Not my Matt, no." I could hear the ice cubes pinging glass as she tipped up her high ball for a sip. "Certainly not." Since she was drunk again, I thought she would have forgotten the whole thing. A week later, a completely stunned Matt called me, explaining that my mother and her police officer husband had busted their way into his dorm room, taken him to a hotel, and interrogated him about his drug usage. After his interrogation, they "treated" him to a steak and lobster dinner before releasing him and leaving campus. It was astounding to me that my mother never lifted a finger to stay in touch with Matt after the divorce, failed to show up in traffic court when he asked for her help, but yet she suddenly "cares" enough to rip him out of his dorm room and educate him about drugs?

The minute I got off the phone with Matt, I called my grandmother. Unfortunately, she answered. The torrent of cusswords I unleashed at her was so loud, two sorority houses called to make sure nothing was wrong.

"You sent that fucking bitch to our campus with her husband?" I screamed, terrified of my own rage and not recognizing my own voice.

"I...I was just trying to help," she said meekly, but I didn't buy it. Now I knew the truth – her behavior was no different than my mother's conniving, manipulation. When I thought about it, I realized when they got together, it was hard to tell where one person stopped and the other started. They agreed on everything and reflected their opinions off each other like two full-length mirrors. Realizing my mother and grandmother were one in the same, cut from the same fabric, and driven by insatiable jealousy, I should have known the day would come when my grandmother would betray me.

"You live to make other people miserable," I yelled, as my voice cracked with tears.

"I'm sorry," she answered quietly. "I'm going to hang up now."

"Fine," I slammed the phone down.

At the time, I conveniently forgot my part in setting my grandmother straight and throwing my brother under the bus. Instead, I focused on my grandmother's betrayal. From that day on, our relationship was never quite the same, although she never dispatched my mother to any family scene again. But still, nothing could take the good memories I had of her raising me when I was little away from me. She dressed me up in straw hats and matching purses, let me play with her jewelry for hours, and took me all over town to lunch, introducing me to everyone, so proud. Not once was she ever too busy to pay attention to me, stopping her dinner preparations to play store with me in the driveway. After the Matt incident, I tucked those memories safely away in my mind and handled the brambles of her alcoholism with thick work gloves.

Meanwhile, my dad arrived in town for Parents' Weekend. We took him out to brunch, ordered bloody marys, and delivered the news. His head dropped. "She invaded your sanctuary," he said sadly. "That bitch." We cheered. From that moment on, my father stopped telling us to talk positive about our mother because, after all, "She is your mother." Sitting there commiserating over what happened felt like we were a family again, just like when we snuck out the back door to escape her. But that moment soon slipped away, leaving us each to deal with the future as grown ups in our own ways. Returning back to my routine after shaking off the sickening feeling that my mother invaded my space, too, took some time. Eventually, I felt safe that my mother really was gone. Then, suddenly she returned.

Walking out of Hanson Hall after earning a 33% on a political science test I studied hard for stopped me in my tracks. "You're a dumb ass," my mother's voice crashed through my mind like a baseball through a window. "You're a failure. You'll always be a failure." I grabbed my head with my hands. My books fell to the floor like dead birds. Another student rushed over to me, thinking I was having a stroke. "I'm okay, I just got dizzy," I lied, terrified that I was a genuine crackpot. After a minute sitting on a bench, I pulled myself together, dismissed the event from my mind, and went back to my life as college girl.

What I had no idea of knowing at the time was that chaos had carved a hole in my psyche. As long as chaos stayed present in my life, the hole remained plugged and allowed me to bob through my life like a rowboat on rippling water. But the minute my life approached normal, the hole ruptured, making me scramble to stuff the hole with something, anything, to save myself from sinking to the bottom. When the thought that I was certifiably insane after hearing my mother's voice in my head lingered, I drowned it with beer. When the fear that I could fail even a quiz surfaced, I studied so obsessively, I forgot to eat. To keep my anxiety from spurting out, I stuffed every day with 21 hours of credit hours, working at a daily newspaper, and heading up a charity golf tournament. And when that didn't work, I entered abusive, wildly unhealthy relationships that filled the hole nicely. Unfortunately, nice guys did not make me comfortable because they flat out failed to deliver the level of destruction I craved.

"Women are bitches; some are pigs," Brad Carter told me. Perfect. That should have been my first clue that Brad wasn't the best choice for a boyfriend. Instead, I fell for Brad's sense of humor and the way he called me "Sweet Dew" and "Golden Palomino," pronouncing the words with a deep southern accent as if each word were heavily coated with syrup. I also fell for his "serious student" looks. Whether Brad went to a Grateful Dead concert or a field party, he dressed in oxford shirts and khaki shorts so heavily starched, they literally stood on their own when he dropped them to the floor. At Grateful Dead shows, people drifted away from him, thinking he was a narc or federal agent. That perception amused him. On campus, he was easily mistaken for a professor. He loved that perception, too.

Soon I discovered projecting false impressions was his specialty. It turned out he wasn't actually a student and had been "dismissed" from the university for doing something horrible he refused to admit to me. So he stayed on campus, living off the money his father gave him for tuition, but never attended school. Technically, he shouldn't have been allowed to participate in the fraternity; but since he had a job at a beer distributor, he was always welcome. By the time I figured out his deception, it was too late. Deeply in love, I thought if he loved me enough, he would straighten out his life and change. Now that would be the ultimate sign of love, I thought. So I tried everything I could to get him to enroll in community college, and he did for a while. But it became clear to me he had no intention of getting a degree, much less creating a life for himself outside of the charade of professional college student.

In the beginning, he scooped me up at all hours to restaurants, fraternity parties, and cookouts at his fraternity brothers' houses. Soon my life meshed with his, and his friends constantly asked, "Are you bringing Jacki? Where's Jacki?" The way he folded me into his chest when he held me, took care of me when I got sick, and snuck dinner into the library for me when I studied, made me cling to him. When he fell apart, I tried to help him. He stopped riding his bike twenty miles a day and started drinking more, which made his stomach bulge out. He made plans with me and never showed up. He made love to me, then tossed me to the floor like a rag doll. When I threatened to leave the relationship, he sent me enormous bouquets of roses, and the mean-nice cycle started all over again, except the time I fell apart.

For a while, the abusive cycle with Brad filled me with just the right amount of chaos. Plus, spending all my energy trying to change him meant I could ignore my own problems. If anyone needed to change, I did. Crying all night seemed both romantic and pathetic, but right somehow, probably because Brad wasn't really what I was crying about. Being lost and having a shaky foundation as faulty as a lean-to shack was more like it. When Brad returned to me, I felt a false sense of confidence. But at night, something broke out of its cage and started chasing me.

At first, I paced around the house all night, but the sensation that something was chasing me from the inside persisted. When I talked to Brad about it, he shoved me away and told me to stop trying to get attention. So, I started driving around all night, flooring my Honda as fast as it would go on the highway, hoping I'd simply crash and die. Killing myself would put an end to the maddening feeling I couldn't escape, but I wanted it to appear as random as "she was speeding and lost control of the car" crash. I didn't want to take responsibility for anything, especially not my own death. Not this time, anyway.

After repeating my late-night driving episodes for months, my weight plunged to 105 pounds, making my head look like an oversized bobble head on a noodle-thin body, and I got mono. A university doctor ordered me to quit all extracurricular activities and narrow down my course load, which removed all of the insulation between me and whatever was chasing me. Suddenly, I was forced to sit still and think. The truth edged closer. Then my roommate, Jan, who happened to be majoring in psychology, noticed. "I'm worried about you," she said. "You're losing too much weight, and God, Jacki, look at your eyes." They were sunken into the sockets, like a Halloween mask. "I'm taking you to Campus Counseling."

Right away, Josie Taylor, the counselor I was assigned to, intimidated me. She flipped through the questionnaire I had checked "Extremely" on every answer and looked at me over her hip black-rimmed glasses that made her look like she was about to conduct a science experiment. She was completely unimpressed. I imagined her rolling her eyes at the problems in my little sorority girl world when there were so many people with real problems. We started talking about the immediate symptoms – weight loss, anxiety, depression, but I held back the "I drive around all night hoping to die" thought. I told her everything else, starting with hearing my mother's voice in my head and my fear that my mother would be right, I'm not smart enough to succeed in school.

"Have you considered if you failed out, it would make your mother feel better about herself failing out?" she said, pushing her wide shoulders back in her chair. My mother had, in fact, failed out of school as a freshman.

"Well, no. But it sounds good," I said.

We talked more about my background and how my mother attacked my every move. She told me I grew up in a "war zone" and probably have some post-traumatic stress going on.

"A past like yours is like acid behind a metal door," she said. "Eventually, the truth will eat through. Yours is eating through now," she said. "You're running from it, but you can't. I'm here to help you face it." A sense of relief washed over me. Maybe I could get some sleep and stop wasting gas.

For the next few months, I saw Josie every week. We explored how having a mother like mine was like having frayed wiring that sometimes works, but still misfires and sparks. We also identified the alcoholic, controlling patterns of her personality: expectations and false images. Every situation had to go exactly as she saw it, or she'd come undone. As for false images, she saw what she wanted to see in herself and others. So when she saw herself in a white dress, she thought she looked like a model; other people thought she looked like a ghost. The unfortunate thing I couldn't see was that I was heading down the same path of alcoholic behavior and abuse. That truth would emerge later. For now, I was too busy twisting therapy into what I needed it to be.

"My mother is useless," I blurted out one day, making Josie explode out of her chair.

"Who are you to call anyone useless? Do you realize how judgmental that is? Who the hell do you think you are?" she blasted me. "Our time is up for today. Just go."

Instead of applying her advice about being judgmental to situations that warranted it, I took it to mean that I shouldn't "judge" anyone's choices, including Brad's. That meant overlooking the way he treated me and the fact that he was pretending to be a college student and asking me to lie to his family.

The fact that Brad treated his dog better than me should have been enough for me to break up with him. Even worse, the fact that his friends not only berated him for treating his dog better, but begged me to leave him, should have convinced me. But it would take more than that to get me to stop clinging on to the chaos and the false image that he was good to me, and we were good together. The relationship would endure one more explosion before settling to a sad dust when Brad suddenly grabbed my arm and ripped me out of the stands at a football game.

"You always do what I say anyway," he snapped, dragging me through the parking lot.

"Get the hell off me," I screamed at him, but he clamped on harder, forcing me into the car and speeding to his apartment. When we got to the door, he shoved me inside.

"You're nothing but a cunt," he yelled at me, eyes wild. I shoved him backwards into the wall, making his Jerry Garcia poster sway behind him. When he straightened up and ducked his head like a bull, I thought he was going to hit me. So I grabbed a kitchen knife and pointed it at him, ready to unleash my rage of being manhandled one too many times by my mother.

"You lay one hand on me, and I'll kill you. You understand me, you son of a bitch?" I said, tightening my grip around the knife. Again, not recognizing my own voice made me shudder. Knowing that I would attack him if he laid one hand on me made my skin crackle with fire. For once, I was taking up for myself. I just wished I wasn't holding a knife. He slumped sadly and started to cry, "I can't believe you think I'm going to hurt you." I kept the knife pointed at him as I backed up to the phone and called Jan to pick me up. I dropped the knife, and his rage returned. He threw the apartment door open and shoved me out in the pouring rain at 2 a.m. Then, he slammed the door and locked it while I stood outside waiting for Jan.

While he had never acted violent before, I still don't have a clear understanding what had happened to him that night. I suspect whatever medication he took every day reacted with the huge amount of whiskey he drank at the game. His extreme mood swings could have been something else entirely, coupled with whatever illegal drugs he took. Miraculously, what he did to me that night still didn't drive me away. Again, I was taken in by his apologies and invitation to the Sunday brunch we went to every week. The fear of being alone and desire to not judge him drove me right back to him. But graduation served to be the ultimate end of our relationship.

Watching other boyfriends stand proudly next to their graduating girlfriends ignited my resolve that I deserved better. That semester, I had challenged myself to earn the only 4.0 I had ever earned, and I did it. I felt sad for myself because, after all that work, I really wanted Brad to be proud of me. For an instant, I spotted Brad in the coliseum. Then, he was gone. Standing there with "Thanks, Dad" scrawled in chalk on my black cap, desperately looking for him in the stands, I finally realized I wanted better for myself. Just then, my dad stood up in the stands. I saw him immediately as if pride had made him ten feet tall. He put me through college. This was his day even more than mine, after everything he sacrificed to get me through college unscathed by loans.

As for Brad, I wasn't sure how I would do better, but I knew I had to find a way. Without the glue college provided to artificially hold my brothers and me together, we drifted apart. As the years went by, the distance hardened into the distrust our mother had once set in motion. My father confirmed that she made a sport out of pitting us against each other, creating a nest of hatred. But my brothers only seemed to have spite, not respect, for me. So I went forward with my life wondering if we might have been friends had our family situation been different.

After I graduated, I decided to create my own life, without my brothers and with a supportive boyfriend. Finding someone held all kinds of promise for building the life I wanted, until whatever was chasing me found my new address.

> "My sanity check bounced."

21 . ONE LAST TRY

Just like all of our previous therapy sessions, my Atlanta therapist Nancy sat in a wing-backed chair; I sat on the sofa. When I casually announced my intention to end my life, Nancy slid to the end of her chair as if it had been tipped. Her turquoise necklace tumbled forward as she locked her eyes in on mine.

"Now you listen to me, you don't have to kill yourself to get the help you need." Tears stung my eyes. "Just try one more thing. You are not alone in this. Here's what we're going to do."

She made an appointment for me to report directly to a local treatment center for an assessment the next morning. Looking back, I'm not sure why she didn't have the police pick me up and take me to a facility right then and there, but she wasn't aware I had been planning my demise for weeks. Mechanically, I drove myself home and went to bed. The next morning, I somehow threw a suit on like always and reported to work. I sat down and closed out all the projects I could. On some level, I must have known I would end up not just reporting to a center, but checking myself in. No matter what happened, I still wanted to do a good job, even if I ended up dying. If Nancy's treatment center idea didn't work, I knew suicide was my only option.

Rick thought nothing of it when I told him I had to leave for an appointment, not knowing I wouldn't be back for two months. I drove myself to the Bradford Treatment Center and met with another counselor after checking everything in the "extremely" column on a questionnaire, just like I did in college. The minute the counselor asked me how I was feeling, the uncontrollable sobbing started. It was as if something had taken over my body; I was unable to dam my raging emotions. She strongly urged me to check myself in for treatment right then, so I agreed even though I was terrified because this private facility cost $1,000 a day with insurance.

She pushed the tiny metal knobs of a lock on the door behind her desk, making it pop open. Walking through the door of the assessment room and into the center felt like being led into jail after admitting my crime that my life was a failure. The hospital looked more like a chain hotel than a jail. Each room had its own air conditioning floor unit, desk, and bathroom with round edges, and a distorted plastic mirror. A glass mirror could be broken and used. The rooms were filled with non-threatening This End Up furniture with cushions in soothing colors.

A nurse with eyes as soft and blue as a receiving blanket put her arm around me and walked me to the women's unit. After snapping a pathetic "Before" Polaroid of me crying, she led me into a room and apologized profusely for what she had to do next: strip-search me. The center's policy was to ensure I didn't bring anything in I could use to harm myself or anyone else. As my suit dropped to the floor, my crying shifted to trembling. Her face grew sadder as she padded me down, continuously apologizing for having to do this. She separated everything out of my purse cleanly into two piles: "sharps," potentially dangerous items like a metal fingernail file and my seashell hair band, and "safe" items, like toothpaste.

After I got dressed, she took me out to a living room where the other women patients in the unit were watching TV, reading, and drawing. There were no people in straightjackets, and no one twirling around, running into walls. Instead, the room looked more like a TV room in a sorority house with grown-up women. The nurse switched off the TV and said, "Everyone, this is Jacki. She's a little scared, so please make her feel welcome." The shaking rippled through me again as I stood there alone. Then, something happened that had never happened to me before. One by one, everyone in the room stopped what she was doing, walked over, and hugged me. Knowing there were other people in the world getting help for whatever was falling apart was as comforting in their lives as swimming in the ocean with people around. People would at least hear your screams if you got in danger. I was used to treading water alone. If you got upset in my family, they just stared at you. Once I cried at my great grandmother's funeral and my aunt snapped, "What's her problem?"

"It's okay, honey," a 65-year-old woman said to me, putting her arm around my shoulders, as I stood there all wooden, not yet knowing how to absorb such support. "We've all been where you are right now."

"Yeah, ain't that the truth," another woman said, making them all laugh. Just when I thought I might be the youngest woman there, a thread of a girl appeared from around a corner with a feeding tube in her nose. She looked like she was about fourteen, but could have been as old as high school age. With olive skin draped around her bony shoulders, you couldn't really guess her age.

"Hi, I'm Isabella," she said, hugging me as her brittle black hair brushed my cheek, as I watched her feeding tube to make sure I didn't touch it. "Oh this?" She pointed to the tube. "Feeding tube. I've got an eating disorder."

"Nice to meet you," was all I could squeeze out of my voice. Later, I found out she was a prima ballerina who became bulimic trying to stay thin for parts. She had survived three cardiac arrests and couldn't even pee without the door open. That way, the nurses could make sure she didn't purge whatever nutrients her body had desperately tried to absorb that day. Just looking at her fragile body made me want to cry, not to mention think I had no problems compared to her. I could barely talk, so I went back to my room and sat there by myself. I tried to close my door, but a nurse appeared immediately. "Honey, you're on 24-hour suicide watch, so we've got to keep your door open," she said apologetically. Embarrassed that I was so pathetic I had to be "watched," I pulled into myself like a hermit crab backing into its shell. At night, she closed the door halfway so I could sleep. Every hour, a wedge of light swept across me as someone opened my door wider and checked on me as part of the suicide watch.

The next day, I woke up in mix of panic and pure dread thinking, "Oh my God. I'm in a mental hospital." I pulled the covers up to my nose and looked around the room. A black and green "Compositions" notebook sat on the desk with my patient number 88345 written on the front and a pen next to it. 88345 identified who I was and how I felt right then —not human, just an empty number. I had been journaling all through my therapy, so writing seemed like the comfortable thing to do. A sheet of inspirational quotes was inside the cover. I started by scribbling a Mark Twain quote: "Man cannot be comfortable without his own approval," on the front. Then, I started my first page with: "I can't believe I put myself in a mental hospital" not realizing that notebook would ultimately change my life.

"Sharps!" someone yelled outside my door, making me jump thinking someone was loose with a knife. Every morning, the patients were allowed to check out "sharps," like a hair dryer, to get dressed for the day. Then, all the sharps were collected, and the day began. The center kept a strict routine going with small blocks of free time in between meals and every kind of therapy imaginable. I soon learned that maintaining a routine imposed order on the depression; sticking to a routine tamed and corralled it with boundaries, which was probably how I managed to function for so long without breaking down. Every day, I had to be sitting at my desk by 8:15 a.m. when the vice president walked by to see who was on time or late. So I kept myself on a strict routine.

I got dressed, sat in my room alone, and heard another "Sharps due" call when a male nurse named Tim knocked softly and came in to talk to me. He pulled the desk chair out, put his foot up on the seat, and leaned his elbow on his knee, as if he were going to tell me a story. Listening required energy I didn't have, so I just stared at him until he blurred.

"You feel like you don't believe in anything, don't you? Like you've lost everything and that there's nothing left to believe in?" I nodded my head yes as I prayed he wouldn't serve up something religious. Thankfully, he didn't.

"If you can find it in yourself to get better, you will. If you believe you won't, you won't. I'm asking you to try to believe in something, anything." He took his foot off the chair and sat down. "Think of yourself like a battery. You've used up your reserve supply and need to recharge. That's what we do here, recharge batteries." He pushed the chair back under the desk, and I forced a slight smile onto my numb face. "I'll be around if you ever need to talk or anything, okay?"

Tears burned lines down my dry skin as I thought about every word he said, especially about believing in something. At the moment, he was right. I didn't believe in anything, especially myself. If my personality were like a house, the breakdown was like a tornado. Only a concrete pad was left behind. At the moment, I stood on the concrete pad wondering what just happened. Week after week, the depression made me feel like I was alone in the empty deep well of a pool. I desperately wanted to join the people I cared about. Although I could see them, they were out of reach. There were no ladders, no diving boards to hoist myself out, just the blank cement walls and hopelessness. I decided that since I had nothing to lose, I would hold onto what he said, which was like being in the same deep end of a pool and trying to pull yourself out with a popsicle stick. I would have to trust him that the stick would be enough. For the rest of the day, I simply followed the routine and did whatever they told me.

After eating breakfast at the cafeteria with our unit, I was told to report to Linda Templeton, the director, to take care of all the necessary and excruciating phone calls to my outside life. Wearing a perfectly pressed suit, Linda acted as professionally as she looked. But I could tell she was also capable of striking laser-precise boundaries with the quickness of a rattlesnake. First, she called my boss, who surprised me with his concern and support. He told her I could take all the time I needed and that my job would still be there for me when I got back. He also said everyone at work was worried because I was so distraught and had been losing an "unhealthy amount of weight." That fact alone must have set off her "possible eating disorder" alarm, because whenever I ate, two or three counselors watched me like crows waiting for me to fumble a drumstick. Two hours later, a huge bouquet of flowers arrived from work, making me cry, but also scared because my perceptions were wrong. I learned my first lesson immediately: My perceptions did not align with reality. Everyone at work did not actually hate me. I just chose to think that.

Next, Linda called Dad. I curled a throw pillow around me thinking he would get mad and insist I had taken therapy too far. Instead, he told her he wanted to fly down right away, but she told him I needed to do this alone. Since my whole life was subject to scrutiny, and I wasn't sure what role my family played in the big picture at that point, I decided to keep everyone at arm's length. Plus, I was pretty sure Dad and April thought I was a nut job. Now that I was in a hospital, it was certifiable. That perception was off, too. Instead of reprimanding me for "taking therapy too far," Dad and April issued solid support. Ultimately, I'd realize my father's denial had nothing to do with me and everything to do with the fact that it was too painful for him to think about the past. He once told me, "That was Life #1; I'm on Life #2 now," which incensed me because that was like saying I didn't exist.

Later, Dad called me during free time and told me not to worry about the money. When I asked him if he was still proud of me, he cried, "Of course I am honey. I just want you to get better." Everyday, evidence of Dad and April's support arrived– cookies from Little Italy in Baltimore, my favorite chocolate, stuffed animals, and enormous bouquets of flowers for my room. But he never truly wanted to understand why I was there, saying, "Are you going to draw me something today," like I was a five-year-old at a day camp. Later when I told him why I put myself in the hospital, he said, "But I thought you were just upset about work." While I was in the hospital, his support and April's gave me a sliver of hope to grasp. When I told him I was horrified that my psychiatrist wanted to put me on anti-depressants immediately, April assured me the prescription could really help me, and I held onto another popsicle stick and believed her. As a pharmaphobe, a person afraid of taking drugs, I had to be convinced there was no other way to recover without medication. I thought taking drugs meant you were taking the easy way out.

Support came sparingly since no one but Trixie and my friend Rich knew what happened. My comedy friends had been calling, leaving jokes on my answering machine like: "Sorry we sent that clown troupe to your house. You can come back now." At my first visitation hour, Trixie drove over with my pillow, clothes, and a tube of Nair because no razors were allowed for obvious reasons. Instead of being sad that I was there, Trixie was relieved and excited. I was happy to see her, but also ashamed until she held me and let me cry all over her.

"Look at it this way, Eberstarker. This is like super-concentrated therapy. Now you'll be able to have the life you always wanted. Think of it as a fresh start, Eberstarker." It was as if someone had just spiked the sun at me. A flash of Trixie made me feel whole again for a half an hour before the darkness of depression enveloped me again. The next night, my friend Rich arrived looking quietly terrified. Rich and I literally did everything together before I consumed myself with comedy– every party, every Braves game, every concert, every Oscar-nominated movie. People asked if we were dating, but we never had that kind of relationship. He was, and still is, one of the best, most compassionate, funniest friends I've ever had. To me, Rich became family from the first time I met him as I stuffed a peanut butter and banana sandwich in my mouth. He laughed and said, "Elvis sandwich. Cool." Lately, he might have noticed my sense of humor had vanished, but probably had no idea things had gotten this bad. I was sure he had never been to a mental hospital before and hoped the silk flower-accented Quality Inn décor made it bearable.

"I don't know what to say." He looked at the carpet. "Are you okay in here?"

"This might turn out to be the best thing that ever happened to me, Rich," I said, explaining the flashbacks and what had happened to me.

"Oh my God, Jacki. I had no idea. I'm so sorry. Whatever you need. I swear, call me." I knew he meant it. He once drove me to the hospital late at night after I had driven myself home after a blood test. The hospital called in a panic asking if I was seeing spots because my electrolytes were depleted, and I was supposedly in danger of going into cardiac arrest. That's the kind of friend he is. I found myself wondering if he too would think I was a nut ball. Then, I realized he thought I was a nut before I got in here.

Trixie was right, the place was super-concentrated therapy. Each day was structured with a full spectrum of pet therapy, art therapy, dance therapy, and therapy therapy. Peppered in between therapy classes, I had sessions with my regular therapist Nancy and other sessions with a psychiatrist named Dr. Rossi. My plan must have involved first processing through all the low-hanging therapy fruit: physically with a psychiatrist, emotionally with Nancy, and mentally, I would learn what the word "healthy" meant.

My psychiatrist was only concerned with the physical effects of the medication. Her task was to get my depression leveled out and get me to realize that depression is a biological, physical problem that needs to be treated, not something you can "cheer up and get over." Unfortunately, it would take at least two weeks to get my serotonin levels elevated to a healthier level. In the meantime, she told me I could start by eating healthier and questioned me about my weight loss. I told her I simply was too tired to go to Piggly Wiggly and God forbid, make myself something to eat. After watching me wolf down two plates of bacon, the eating disorder fear had been abandoned. If I had employed a personal chef, I wouldn't have lost a pound, I told her.

Emotionally, Nancy helped me sort through and process the series of sexual abuse flashbacks. We started with the night of the flashbacks. So many questions swirled around in my mind. I couldn't understand why the article about Father Connor would set the flashbacks in motion. Nancy explained when you're depressed, everything and anything towers over you, overwhelms, and consumes you. A parking ticket, sideways glance, or change of plans could do it. In my case, learning our family priest was a molester was the last straw, even though I have no memory of him ever touching me. It doesn't make sense why that was the last straw, but it just was.

Talking about the flashbacks felt like trying to run underwater. Each memory played back in slow, excruciating motion, making me relive every second. Soon I would learn that putting yourself through a memory is like walking through a room of demons. Each time you walk through that room, the demons get weaker. As you process through flashbacks, the demons turn to dust, leaving you with more power than you had before, and granting you the unexpected benefit of peace. Only then can you move on to the absolute luxury of worrying about trivial things, like who was the better Darrin on *Bewitched*.

When we talked about my sixth grade experience of Derek O'Leary grabbing me under the table, I distinctly remembered how the pinch of his fingers felt every bit as the air that whistled out of my mouth in pure relief when my teacher told me his family moved. Then, she cheerfully said, "Well, you're going to have to find a new friend to play horse with." Like I was ever going to play that game again. That explained my paralyzing fear of having to play basketball in gym.

As for the memories of Peter, I shuddered realizing he had molested me repeatedly for four years and wondering how so many memories could be completely shrouded in my memory. It was as if my mind had been placed on a diet, feeding itself in small doses until it built up the appetite to handle the main course. Peter's behavior the last time I saw him at Christmas suddenly made sense. I remembered feeling confused because normally, he would have asked me how things were going in Atlanta. Before I moved to Atlanta, he told me: "I don't even have to wonder if you'll make it there, Jacki. I know you will," leaving me with a burst of confidence I held close. Instead, he physically avoided me and refused to make eye contact. He had since married and had several children, including girls. I wondered if he molested the girls? Did he molest neighborhood girls? Was I the only one? Why me? Why didn't I tell someone? Maybe because I didn't just want his attention, I needed it.

The whole thing felt so bittersweet because the Graysons were so good to me, I felt like I didn't have a right to be angry that this happened. It would take a while for me to realize no matter how nice they were to me, I didn't deserve to be molested. No one does. I wondered if Peter gave any thought to the fact that one day, his little toy would grow up. One day, I'd remember. And one day, I'd tell. I got the feeling his arrogance made him think otherwise. Nancy quickly redirected my questions about Peter with: "We'll deal with him. Let's get back to you."

Although nowhere near as ongoing as Peter's abuse, the flashback that disturbed me the most involved Mr. Hagwood. Why did he have to do that? Did he help me get through eighth grade so he could later make a move on me? Was that his motivation all along? Was he scared I'd tell? Later I told my Addison Junior High friend Jenny what happened, and she said, "That pig." Then, she made sure she mentioned my name about twenty times when she ran into him at a bookstore. She said he physically squirmed. What could have been one of those heart-warming stories about how a teacher turned a kid's life around turned to shit instead. I felt robbed because I thought he cared about me, but I guess he really only wanted something else. Then, I wondered what his wife would have thought had she known about his methods of delivering holiday greetings.

When we moved into my behavior of offering myself up to a boy in eighth grade and earning the nickname "school slut" for good reason, I slumped. Feeling like everyone else was in charge of my destiny except me felt so pathetic. But instead of allowing the name "slut" to be branded into my soul like it used to be,

I realized that at that age, my actions were a cry for help more than an indication of who I really was. I did things like that out of desperation to be accepted. It made me realize when girls act promiscuously; they're lost and desperately need help. I was one of those girls, but I kept it to myself. The more adult behavior of entering into an affair with Paul was a lot harder to take. "The man was a pedophile, Jacki. You're assuming too much responsibility for that," Nancy said. Even though I was eighteen, Nancy convinced me not to take full ownership and responsibility for that situation. Even now, I struggle with understanding the dual nature of someone who is supportive, yet predatory.

At night, the angry dark-haired girl dominated my dreams. I wondered who she was or whom she represented. When we worked on "learning to become whole" by connecting with our inner children, her identity became clear. During a relaxation exercise, I visualized myself alone on a porch on a beach when a funny child with golden hair bounced up wearing a pretty flower dress. She must have represented the part of myself that everyone described as "deliriously happy." Then, a child with dark hair showed up. She was wearing a grubby dress, and her face had dirt smudged all over it. I realized she was the same dark-haired girl who frequented my dreams before I came here, the one who hated me. In another exercise, we opened a dialogue with our "inner children" by writing a question with our dominant hand in our journals and an answer with our non-dominant hand.

"Dear Dark Inner Child, please come and talk to me. I want to get to know you."

"Why don't you love me? Why did you abandon me? I didn't do anything mean to you. I loved you, but you didn't love me. Only golden child- she's more fun than me."

"You are a mystery to me. Who are you?"

"I'm more aggressive than you, but you never let me play. You are afraid of me. I want you to love me, but I'm mad at you because you act like I don't exist."

"I'm sorry. I didn't know I abandoned you. I need you to help me get through. Please know I do love you."

The more I worked with communicating with my inner children, the more everything made sense. The dark child absorbed all the sexual abuse and stayed hidden all that time. The light-haired inner child represented the comedian side of myself. Nancy encouraged me to integrate both parts of myself to "becoming whole" and heal. I wrote letters to myself in my journal explaining that I was sorry and that I forgave myself for my choices. I drew pictures of Dark Inner Child holding a heart and Light Inner Child holding flowers, then encompassed them with a circle.

"You have two inner children?" another patient said, looking at my drawing.

"Yes."

"You're an MPD too," she said, like "I knew it!" I was expecting her to high-five another patient and collect money like they had a bet.

"I am not." I got so freaked out, I went straight to my Nancy in a panic. "Another patient told me I have multiple personality disorder because I have two inner children," I said, sounding like a tattling five-year-old.

"You do not," she laughed. "Don't listen to other patients." *They're crazy.*

After processing through the sexual abuse, some mysteries started to make sense. All through my life, I shredded the skin on my fingers without even realizing it. Sometimes, they'd bleed, so I'd jam them in my pockets. But the blood would soak through the denim. I'd try wrapping Band-Aids around the wounds, but then I'd pick through those. As a result, scar tissue surrounded my thumbs and my nails rippled. Nancy called this behavior "self mutilation" and told me it was a common side effect of someone who has been sexually abused. When Nancy called me a "survivor," I felt the first spark of hope.

"Survivor" sounded valiant, as if I had conquered cancer or perhaps a hurricane. But I also liked the way that word felt a whole lot better than "victim." From that moment on, I told myself I was going to learn how to be a "survivor," not a victim. My therapist issued a challenge: Start acting like a survivor and stop shredding your fingers. So that's what I did, making it through one whole day without touching them. By the time I left the center, my fingers had completely healed. That one step delivered the empowerment of simply making a choice I needed to start turning everything around. For the first time, I felt like I could return to my life and suicidal despair had evaporated.

Meanwhile, hearing the pain in the older women's voices around me filled me with intense appreciation and hope that I could forge the life I wanted. They were distraught that they could have lived completely different lives as recovered, new-and-improved versions of themselves. I paid close attention to what they were saying, realizing how lucky I was to have a breakdown now. I had years ahead of me whereas many of the women cried thinking about the time they had lost. But not everyone in the hospital shared the same desire to get back to her life, I'd discover.

After sitting in the TV room listening to the older women talk about their stories, I went back to my room and discovered I had a roommate.

"Hey, I'm Cassie," a young woman said as she pulled clothes out of her backpack. I wondered why she was here because she seemed happy to be there, which puzzled me. We exchanged typical roommate banter, like where are you from, and avoided the "So, what are you in for?" When we went to dinner with our unit, patients from other tables were high-fiving Cassie, saying, "Hey, what's up? Welcome back." Cassie was most popular in the center. She turned out to be a regular, sharing tricks with me, like making herself barf and demanding a feeding tube so she could stay in longer. "You want to stay in here?" I asked.

"It's better to live here." I didn't know what to say about that, so I just distanced myself. Only when we got around to discussing our "boyfriends" did the similarities make themselves apparent. Cassie's boyfriend Tony had thrown her down a stairwell in New York, then fired a gun at her. She broke her leg, but the bullets missed her. Her father had rescued her from Tony several times, only for Cassie to run straight back to him. After sharing story after story laced with violence and the "boyfriends'" habits of assuring our nothingness, I began to identify the pattern. The stories were so similar, you could have drawn a blank for my current boyfriend's name and simply interchanged the names. You could even fill Tony's name in the blank, the results would be the same. Cassie, too, suffered from postcard traumatic stress disorder, hanging onto the time Tony had taken care of her when she had the flu, and how he helped her get her first job. When Nancy popped her head in our door, Cassie said, "Hey Nancy!"

"You two know each other?" I asked Nancy on the way out.

"Oh yes, she's a career treatment center goer," Nancy said, rolling her eyes.

"Be careful not to take what she says too seriously. Have you heard of the term 'Master Manipulator?'"

Since Nancy had helped me move out of the danger range and gain some peace about the sexual abuse, it was time to deal with the one admission I did not want to deal with – that I focused on seriously demented relationships with guys like Aston to avoid dealing with myself. Nancy told me the clinical word for that behavior – codependency. "I am not Stuart Smalley," I asserted, recalling the whiny *Saturday Night Live* character who looked in the mirror reciting: "I'm good enough, I'm smart enough, and doggone it, people like me." Clutching my postcard of how Aston loved me, I called him for support. He immediately blamed me for the fact that he had been sitting alone in his apartment holding the same gun that he lent me to his head.

"I'm not the one checking myself into a loony bin," he told me, followed by crying how he loved me and couldn't survive without me. "I need my girlfriend, and she's in a fucking loony bin."

"Maybe you should be in here," I said.

"Fuck you," he said back, lovingly. Then, hung up.

Even though I believed it when people said he was toxic to me, the flawed image I had of him being a supportive person who loved me crept back into my thoughts. Even after that vicious exchange, I physically ached for him to hold me and love me the way drug addicts describe needing a fix. The next day, I called Nancy. "Okay, I'm codependent, damn it."

Cassie and I were both ordered to attend a group session for codependents. We slumped down in our chairs as other members of the group described completely ignoring themselves while tending to the lives of people who were not boyfriends, girlfriends, or friends. The group taught me patterns I hated to admit I exhibited, such as: "My good feelings about who I am stem from being liked by you. I am extremely loyal, remaining in harmful situations too long. I accept sex when I want love." As much as I hated going to the codependent group, it made something click in my mind. I began seeing myself as a genuinely nice person putting herself through terrible relationships for no good reason.

Having this thought enabled me to develop self-empathy and recognize the deep sadness in my heart that I just kept doing this to myself. Visualizing my inner children being subject to this behavior made it a lot easier for me to change my dependence on guys like Aston. Luckily, the hospital staff and everyone there was on to me. Whenever I talked about how much I missed Aston, they reminded me how toxic he was. If another patient shared stories that glorified drinking, the staff shut her down too. It was as if I could have substituted the word Aston for cocaine or alcohol. He was the distraction to my problems. It was time for me take responsibility for myself by focusing on myself only.

The next day, Dr. Rossi found me, I thought, to discuss my medication. We sat outside under a tree to talk. After being in the hospital for two weeks, she informed me that my insurance company only covered long-term hospital care to patients who were suicidal. But because I was no longer suicidal, the insurance company said the hospital had to release me. I started crying in fear immediately.

"But I'm not ready. Should I do something suicidal so I can stay longer?" Terrified to go back out into the world, I panicked. She told me I was not to return to work, but enroll in the outpatient program at the center for the next month, which would teach me valuable "survival skills" I would need to go back out into the world.

That night, I played my comedy video to the women in the unit that Trixie had brought over for me. The patients laughed hysterically, but the nurses frowned, saying, "Jacki, you know the difference between what's funny and what's not now, don't you?" I froze because I really didn't. Plus, what would I do with my comedy set now? Would I be able to go back to stand-up? I wasn't sure, but I knew I had to be careful navigating between what was funny and what was destructive.

The next morning, I reluctantly gathered the stuffed animals from Dad and April, pillow, composition notebook, and clothes Trixie brought me from home as Cassie watched.

"Man, I can't believe they're making you leave," Cassie said. "You know what you could do? You could go throw up. Or I know, bash your head against the wall a bunch of times." I just looked at her and kept packing.

"You can keep the flowers," I said since she didn't have any.

The nurse with the soft-blue eyes snapped an "After" Polaroid of me, smiling this time. Then, she hugged me and told me she was proud of the work I had done there. I found myself wishing she were my mom. I cried when I said goodbye to the other women who were so supportive of me and wished them the best. A receptionist at the front door pushed the metal buttons, and I walked out in the glaring sun to my car alone. Just like I came.

As I watched Isabella and other patients reunite with their families and husbands, I felt sad I was leaving by myself, yet empowered by a pang of triumph. I had been walking down the wrong street all along, falling in the same hole over and over again. This time, I chose a different street.

ACKNOWLEDGEMENTS

Thank you...

Gary G., Elizabeth W. and Debba W. for believing in me when I didn't.

Jodianne D. for years of enduring friendship punctuated by one week of grueling work on the amazing book design.

LG and Shark for years of mutual respect and applause.

Paula and Mark H. for the tidal surge of enthusiasm that pushed the book to completion.

Anne B. for staying my dedicated friend through it all.

Dad for suppressing the urge to flee and staying with your kids instead.

Len for offering your wisdom and support at all hours.

Dorothy C. for fueling me with love only a great mom could deliver.

My late grandmother Rosemarie for planting seeds of confidence that finally took root.

Brian for unwavering support that brings out brilliance.

S and L for showing me the true meaning of family, not to mention comedy.

I love you all.

Sass Mouth
DESTINY IS A JOKE

A memoir by Jacki Kane

Meet Jacki Eberstarker, a girl who grows up in Baltimore defying her police officer mother while clenching a Bionic Woman doll. Raised to be as powerless as a household object, she flounders through life falling into every trap along the way - disastrous relationships, alcohol abuse, and a debilitating fear of clowns. As she finds success in stand-up comedy, devastating truths emerge that nearly destroy her. SASS MOUTH is a story about taking responsibility, blasting through a faulty foundation, and proving that, ultimately, happiness is the best revenge.

Photo @ Colleen Cahill

Jacki Kane is an award-winning copywriter and host of *TIME OUT: The mother of all comedy shows*. Combining her stand-up material and life as crazed parent, she created Sass Mouth Cards, a line of smarty pants greeting cards. She lives in Portland, Oregon, with her husband and two children. Visit her at jackikane.wordpress.com.

Sass Mouth DESTINY IS A JOKE
A memoir by Jacki Kane

ISBN 978-0-557-13520-2